Education and Poverty

STUDIES IN SOCIAL ECONOMICS

Education and Poverty

Thomas I. Ribich

THE BROOKINGS INSTITUTION
Washington, D.C.

THE BROOKINGS INSTITUTION is an independent organization devoted to non-partisan research, education, and publication in economics, government, foreign policy, and the social sciences generally. Its principal purposes are to aid in the development of sound public policies and to promote public understanding of issues of national importance.

The Institution was founded on December 8, 1927, to merge the activities of the Institute for Government Research, founded in 1916, the Institute of Economics, founded in 1922, and the Robert Brookings Graduate School of Economics and Government, founded in 1924.

The general administration of the Institution is the responsibility of a self-perpetuating Board of Trustees. The trustees are likewise charged with maintaining the independence of the staff and fostering the most favorable conditions for creative research and education. The immediate direction of the policies, program, and staff of the Institution is vested in the President, assisted by an advisory council chosen from the staff of the Institution.

In publishing a study, the Institution presents it as a competent treatment of a subject worthy of public consideration. The interpretations and conclusions in such publications are those of the author or authors and do not purport to represent the views of the other staff members, officers, or trustees of the Brookings Institution.

Foreword

Despite the common faith in education as a method of alleviating poverty, very little has been done to quantify the potential contribution of education to the war on poverty. This methodological study explores the feasibility of measuring the income gains resulting from improved education. Several types of education are evaluated by comparable measures of efficiency, and the resulting estimates are contrasted. The estimates are supplemented with an analysis of the problems of evaluating the benefits of special education programs.

The author is especially grateful to William M. Capron, Rashi Fein, and Joseph A. Pechman who provided an unusual amount of encouragement and advice throughout this study. He also wishes to thank Alice M. Rivlin and Joseph D. Mooney for their discerning comments on earlier drafts of the manuscript. Martin C. Carnoy, Edward F. Denison, Herbert J. Kiesling, Henry M. Levin, Robert W. Rafuse, Jr., and Theodore W. Schultz made many helpful suggestions. The manuscript also benefited from the comments of an advisory group consisting of Raymond Breton, Jesse Burkhead, Richard S. Eckhaus, Robinson Hollister, Robert A. Levine, Alexander M. Mood, Joseph D. Mooney, and Burton A. Weisbrod, in addition to Mrs. Rivlin and Messrs. Capron and Fein. The cooperation of William W. Cooley and John C. Flanagan of Project Talent made possible the tabulations of some important unpublished data. Ann Rosenthal and Margaret Donaldson were helpful research assistants. The manuscript was edited by Alice M. Carroll and the index prepared by Rachel M. Johnson.

The study was prepared with the financial support of a grant by the Carnegie Corporation. The views expressed in the study are those of the author and are not represented as the views of the Carnegie Corporation or the staff members, officers, or trustees of the Brookings Institution.

KERMIT GORDON
President

August 1968
Washington, D.C.

Contents

TABLES

CHAPTER I

Education as an Investment

A major presumption of the war on poverty is that education and training are especially effective ways to bring people out of poverty. How well founded is this presumption? Which types of education are most productive? This study develops techniques that may help to answer such questions and it suggests the direction such answers may take.

The basic analytical technique used in this study is benefit-cost analysis, an approach that represents economics in one of its most venturesome moods. To many noneconomists, however, the technique suggests the replacement of wisdom with a limited mechanical procedure. To many economists it appears to rest too much on the unsteady foundation of theoretical welfare economics.

But with public policy already committed to a war on poverty, many of the standard objections to benefit-cost procedures have reduced force. The first aim of the war, after all, can be viewed as essentially an economic one of raising the incomes of the poor. This makes the task of benefit-cost analysis a great deal easier. For while such computations can never hope to give an accurate weighing to all advantages and disadvantages, they can measure reasonably well the economic impact on the directly affected individuals.

A related advantage of working within the context of a war on poverty is that the poverty program gives the economist some guide to income distribution preferences. The implicit consensus of a publicly sponsored antipoverty campaign is that one group, the individuals in poverty, have greater "need" for additional income than do other people. Thus the usual agnosticism of the theoretical welfare economist on redistribution questions seems inappropriate in this instance. A dollar gain for the poor at the cost of less than a dollar for the average taxpayer apparently brings a net gain for society. Dollar amounts thus become an unusually good proxy for the underlying notion of overall economic welfare, and the comparison of dollar benefits with dollar costs becomes directly relevant for policy questions.

Before specific computations can be undertaken in a benefit-cost framework, several conceptual and methodological issues must be resolved. To set the stage, some straightforward applications of the economics of education are reviewed.

The Simple Case for Education

In the history of economic thought, education has consistently been a favored means of social improvement, especially for the poor. Economists' enthusiasm for education has at times brought together strange bedfellows. Adam Smith and Karl Marx both emphasized the critical need for improved education in developing general aptitudes among working men as well as in countering the erosion of public responsibility brought on by the division of labor. Malthus and Ricardo, though frequently at odds, agreed that more education was required to improve the moral fiber of the lower classes.[1]

Many of the arguments for the public support of education are based on the observation that education is of great benefit to society in general and not just to the specific individuals who are educated. But this does not help in answering the question of whether an additional expenditure on education at this point in time is an efficient way of raising the incomes of the poor.[2] What is needed

[1] For a survey of eighteenth and nineteenth century economic comments on education, see John Vaizey, *The Economics of Education* (Free Press, 1962), pp. 15-25.

[2] Social benefits—or, to use the technical term, "external" benefits—do, of course, have relevance when it comes to making final decisions about the appropriate magnitude and types of education. Thus, even though the focus of this study is on the

instead is a reason why individuals undertake less educational investment in themselves than is warranted by the personal rate of payoff to education.

HUMAN CAPITAL INVESTMENT

The most general reason that can be provided relies on the idea of an inherent capital market imperfection that holds back *all* forms of human investment, not only education. Milton Friedman argues:

If a fixed money loan is made to finance investment in physical capital, the lender can get some security for his loan in the form of a mortgage or residual claim to the physical asset itself, and he can count on realizing at least part of his investment in case of necessity by selling the physical asset. If he makes a comparable loan to increase the earning power of a human being, he clearly cannot get any comparable security; in a non-slave state, the individual embodying the investment cannot be bought and sold.[3]

Thus, among equally expensive things a poor person might wish to purchase with borrowed funds, a tangible and resalable item is most attractive to the lender. The prospective financier is more apt to be interested if the contemplated investment is a building or a machine rather than an equally costly course of study. The upshot is apparent: in terms of benefits to individuals, there is a tendency for less than an optimal amount to be invested in human capital.

With borrowing made difficult, the individual himself can, of course, postpone investment until his savings accumulate. Unfortunately, the peculiarities of human capital make such postponement unusually expensive; for if a man in pursuit of education withdraws from the labor force, his loss in wages can be quite heavy.[4] But a perhaps more pervasive problem is the reduction

---

limited question of the efficiency of education in raising the income of the poor, externalities are examined in detail in Chap. 6.

[3] Milton Friedman, "The Role of Government in Education," in Robert A. Solo (ed.), *Economics and the Public Interest* (Rutgers University Press, 1955), p. 137. The first clear statement of the idea appears to be A. C. Pigou, *The Economics of Welfare* (4th ed.; Macmillan, 1932), pp. 746-47.

[4] See J. R. Walsh, "Capital Concept Applied to Man," *Quarterly Journal of Economics*, Vol. 49 (1935), pp. 255-85. Increasing family responsibilities also make any temporary belt-tightening more painful.

in total lifetime return on his investment. The absence of resale value for human capital means that the investment is income-yielding only so long as the original investor lives. The contrast with investments in physical capital is readily apparent. Once a factory, for instance, is constructed and turned into a profitable venture, the capitalized value of the future earnings stream can be sold and the original entrepreneur can depart, taking with him a large share of an income stream that continues to be generated despite his absence. For education there is no parallel option.

In short, when human capital is the contemplated investment, the individual with little cash finds himself in a dilemma. If he tries to plunge ahead immediately, he encounters a hostile capital market and very high interest rates (should he be fortunate enough to find a creditor). If he delays, rising opportunity costs and a shortened stream of returns begin to close in. Thus, allowing the possibility of postponement seems only to heighten the difference between physical and human capital. For the individual the pressures still play against educational investment.

But analyzing the behavior of a single individual trying to make an investment choice—human versus physical—understates the difference between the two forms of investment.

The trouble with the example of the lone unaffluent young person is the temptation to conclude that the only thing that separates human and physical investment is the *ease* of postponement. This indeed is the suggestion of Gary Becker's argument that an eighteen-year-old who tries to invest in physical capital, rather than advanced education, would have nearly the same borrowing difficulties. Becker points out that the "collateral provided by his equipment would probably be very imperfect"; and the young man's only consolation is that he "might, without too much cost, postpone the investment for a number of years until his reputation and equity were sufficient to provide the 'personal' collateral required to borrow funds."[5] But is there any real cost at all? The young man of course loses something by being rebuffed in his early borrowing attempt, but this is inadequate proof that the in-

[5] Gary S. Becker, *Human Capital* (National Bureau of Economic Research, 1964), p. 58.

vestment itself will be postponed and that a net loss *for society* occurs.

Indeed, there is very good reason to suspect that society does *not* suffer on balance. The youth who cannot exploit a particular physical investment is likely to find that the investment opportunity does not wait for him. If the contemplated investment (for example, a new factory) is truly profitable, chances are a well-established man will take advantage of it, and the implied increase in productivity will be realized with little delay. Thus the problems of youth and poverty need not imply any lag at all in the rate of physical investment; and the rate of return on such investment should, therefore, remain reasonably close to the interest rate at which the most trustworthy in the community can borrow. In human investment, however, the young man who could profit greatly from his investment in education is also a vital part of the investment opportunity. If he delays (or fails altogether to acquire) his education, the delayed (or missed) opportunity cannot be exploited by another, more seasoned investor. For the productivity gain to be realized, the young man must personally engage in an act of investment.

This difference can be brought into clearer focus by considering Marshall's observation that business ability is positively related to the ownership of physical capital, and skilled entrepreneurs will therefore control great amounts of such capital.[6] Becker applies this to suggest a parallel between human and physical investment: namely, that relatively bright people tend to invest relatively more in themselves.[7] But there would seem to be a very sharp divergence in this parallel. For physical capital, it is apparent that a relatively small group of specialized individuals can exploit a vast proportion of the available opportunities in an economy—there is hardly a limit on the number of good business sites that an able businessman can purchase and use. On the other hand, an able investor in human capital has, so to speak, only one business site at his disposal: his own talent. Only a limited amount of capital

---

[6] Alfred Marshall, *Principles of Economics* (9th ed.; Macmillan, 1961), Vol. 1, p. 312.

[7] Becker, *Human Capital*, p. 63.

can be "erected" on this "site." This means that, in the case of education, the exploitation of all good "sites" requires investment activities by multitudes of people, many of whom have weak collateral and poor market knowledge.[8]

This is not to say that the prospective eighteen-year-old businessman in Becker's example is no worry at all. When financiers fail to trust youthful businessmen, it can be inferred that the supply of entrepreneurial talent is restricted, tending to drive up the price of entrepreneurial services and thereby to curtail the total number of physical investments undertaken. But given the fact that a single experienced businessman can successfully initiate a large number of projects, there is doubt that this is a serious concern.[9] Moreover, there is reason to think that the supply of skilled businessmen is largely a problem of *human* capital. Perhaps the eighteen-year-old would do well to get a degree in industrial management rather than thrashing around in the business world until his "personal" collateral builds up.

The various aspects of the embodiment problem in human capital can thus be understood best as a deductive chain: (1) for a given individual, human capital is exceptionally poor collateral to offer a prospective creditor; (2) an effort to avoid borrowing, by waiting until savings accumulate, turns out to be an expensive proposition and can deter human capital investments once the early oppor-

[8] A number of early discussions come close to this argument. Marshall himself notes that "the action of competition, and the survival in the struggle for existence . . . tend in the long run to put the building of factories and steam engines in the hands of those who will be ready and able to incur every expense which will add more than it costs to their value as productive agents. But the investment of capital in the rearing and early training of the workers of England is limited by the resources of parents in the various grades of society. . . ." (Marshall, *Principles of Economics*, p. 561.) See also Wesley C. Mitchell, "The Backward Art of Spending Money," *American Economic Review*, Vol. 2 (1912), pp. 269-81; and Pigou, *The Economics of Welfare*, p. 274. Our argument differs mainly in its explicit connection with the general problem of "embodied" investment.

[9] Marshall, despite his somber worries about underinvestment in education, is quite sanguine about the supply of entrepreneurial services. "[There are] many routes . . . by which a man of great natural business ability can work his way up high in some private firm or public company, [and] we may conclude that wherever there is work on a large scale to be done in such a country as England, the ability and the capital required for it are pretty sure to be speedily forthcoming." (*Principles of Economics*, p. 312.)

tunity is missed; (3) in contrast, postponement by an individual of an investment in physical capital does not usually mean that the investment itself is neglected or that the rate of return is substantially influenced; and (4) there is no market tendency for human investment decisions to become effectively specialized and centralized. The implication is essentially the same as before: natural market forces tend to keep the rate of return on human capital well above that on other investments, creating the presumption that education is an especially efficient way of intervening to help the poor.

It may well be that the embodiment problem (and its logical consequences) is only a minor factor influencing educational attainment and educational expenditures. For instance, the "subculture of poverty" may be the most important factor in explaining and predicting individual educational decisions among the poor[10] and in determining whether added educational investments are appropriate. The poor may have biases against the classroom that lead them to systematically underrate the power of education, thus implying that society should counter this "irrationality" by greatly increasing its efforts on the education front. But it may be that the poor will not respond effectively to education unless poverty itself is first ameliorated. Though research on the social and psychological attributes of the poor is illuminating,[11] there is little agreement on whether (on balance) the existence of a subculture of poverty weakens or strengthens the case for education.

Another, more obvious facet of the educational investment problem is the heavy social support of education already in existence. This force surely operates to raise the total investment in education above what it would otherwise be. The issue can be simply reduced to the question of whether or not the present level of subsidization is sufficient to overcome the "natural" tendencies toward underinvestment in education. The answer to this ques-

---

[10] For discussion of this subject see Frank Riessman, *The Culturally Deprived Child* (Harper & Row, 1962), and Kenneth Clark, *Dark Ghetto* (Harper & Row, 1965), Chap. 5.

[11] Much of the research is designed to give teachers and school administrators the necessary empathy to reach children with poor backgrounds; for a review of the literature see Benjamin S. Bloom, Allison Davis, and Robert Hess, *Compensatory Education for Cultural Deprivation* (Holt, Rinehart & Winston, 1965).

tion is not apparent. If there is a tendency for the public sector to receive less than an optimal allotment of resources, the counterbalancing force of subsidization is likely to be insufficient. Moreover, the poor, being a politically weak minority group, may receive less than a "fair share" of expenditures in the public sector. On the other hand, since education is publicly valued for many reasons other than the private income gained by those educated, education may already receive fiscal support far in excess of what could be justified in terms of financial profitability. The current level of support may be more than is necessary to counteract the capital market barriers to private educational investment. If this is true, the rate of return to education may already be very low and the attempt to raise private incomes via added education may even entail costs in excess of the resulting pure financial gain. In that case, further expansion of education would be an expensive way to bring people out of poverty.

The net effect of these opposing forces cannot be reckoned by casual observation and inference. Actual measurement of gains and costs is required. Several studies have attempted to do this.

THE PAYOFF RATE FROM CONTINUED EDUCATION

For the most part, the empirical studies testing the hypothesis of underinvestment in education have concentrated on estimating the payoff rate for continuing formal education through an additional block of years. The aim is to measure how profitable it is for an average student to attend an additional two (or perhaps four) years in the regular educational sequence, and to judge whether this payoff rate is high enough to justify the encouragement of heavier flows of students through these levels of schooling.[12] Thus far, indications are that the payoff is sufficiently high. Those who attempt to make an empirical case for giving education a large role

[12] See Theodore W. Schultz, "Education and Economic Growth," in Nelson B. Henry (ed.), Social Forces Influencing American Education (University of Chicago Press, 1961); Becker, Human Capital; W. Lee Hansen, "Total and Private Rates of Return to Investment in Schooling," Journal of Political Economy, Vol. 71, No. 2 (April 1963), pp. 128-40; and Giora Hanoch, "Rates of Return, 1960," University of Chicago, Office of Agricultural Research, Paper No. 6428, Nov. 12, 1964 (unpublished).

in the battle against poverty generally rely upon this evidence.[13] The payoff rates calculated in the school continuation studies are sometimes in the form of discounted benefits as a ratio of costs, but more often they are expressed as internal rates of return specifying the rate of discount necessary to equate returns with costs. Both "private" and "social"[14] rates of return have been computed. The former equate estimated after-tax lifetime income gain with personal costs borne by the individual who continues his education. The latter equate before-tax gains with the total resource costs of the extra years of education, regardless of who pays what part of the bill. Though many differences can be found in computational technique and in final tallies, practically all of the studies arrive at the conclusion that the payoff rate for continued education at all levels is remarkably high—something in excess of 10 percent for college education and perhaps as high as 50 percent for increments at lower levels.[15] On both a private and a social basis, the empirical consensus suggests that increasing the flow of students at any level is an investment whose costs are easily covered by the anticipated financial benefits.

Although this result is widely accepted and frequently cited, a number of critics have suggested that the conceptual difficulties involved in estimating the returns to education are serious enough to undermine a pro-education conclusion.[16] Some critics question

[13] See Committee for Economic Development (CED), *Raising Low Incomes Through Improved Education* (CED, 1965), pp. 16, 17; Theodore W. Schultz, "Investing in Poor People: An Economist's View," *American Economic Review*, Vol. 55, No. 2 (May 1965), pp. 515-16; and Michael S. March, "Poverty: How Much Will the War Cost?" *Social Service Review*, Vol. 39 (June 1965), pp. 141-56.

[14] The "social" rate of return referred to here is *not* an estimate of all social benefits produced by education, but the lifetime personal income differentials produced by various amounts of education.

[15] Hanoch, using 1960 census data, derives rates well above 50 percent for some educational increments below the high school level ("Rate of Return, 1960," Table 1, pp. 14-15). Burton A. Weisbrod ("Education and Investment in Human Capital," *Journal of Political Economy*, Vol. 70, No. 5, Supplement [October 1962], pp. 111-12) argues that the 35 percent rate computed by Schultz (*Social Forces Influencing American Education*) for primary school education should be raised to 54 percent because of the "option value" associated with being able to attend higher levels of schooling as a result of successfully completing a lower level. For the rationale behind the "option value" estimate and a critique of it, see App. C.

[16] See Edward F. Renshaw, "Estimating the Returns to Education," *Review of Economics and Statistics*, Vol. 42, No. 3 (August 1960), pp. 318-24; Harry Shaffer,

how much more a person really earns because of the *independent* influence of extra education. The trained individual does not, like a business investment, generate a directly observable profit. As a proxy for actual returns, we can compare the lifetime income stream of a person who manages to complete a given number of school years with that of a person who terminated sooner. The difference between the two streams is the proxy. Unfortunately, those who depart at an earlier point in the educational sequence are not precise counterparts of the people who continue, and in fact are typically less able as students and, presumably, as workers. Consequently, they are likely destined for relatively lower incomes in any event. Therefore, the observed and unadjusted income differentials are probably inflated estimates.

As long as returns estimates are based on income differentials between individuals who continue schooling and those who do not, there will never be a completely adequate answer to this criticism. It can always be asserted that students who opt for continuation are blessed with character traits that might elude even the most skillfully designed objective tests. Nevertheless, considerable progress has been made during the last few years in controlling for at least the tangible differences—in aptitudes and in social and personal characteristics—between individuals who terminate schooling at different levels.

The most notable work along these lines has been performed by Becker.[17] He estimates that the unadjusted private rate of return for going to college, calculated at 13 percent, is reduced to something greater than 11 percent after making all the adjustments permitted by the available information. The more sketchy data relating to lower levels of educational attainment deter his attempts at similar formal adjustments for these levels. He does note, however, that the available clues point to a slightly greater adjustment factor for these levels; but since unadjusted payoff rates are much higher, he concludes that the adjustments would still leave these

---

"Investment in Human Capital: Comment," *American Economic Review*, Vol. 51, No. 5 (December 1961), pp. 1026-35; and R. S. Eckaus, "Economic Criteria for Education and Training," *Review of Economics and Statistics*, Vol. 46, No. 2 (May 1964), pp. 181-90.

[17] *Human Capital*, especially pp. 79-90, 125-26.

rates at enticingly high levels. More refined empirical work remains to be done on this question. Still, the small effect of the readily measurable characteristics has shifted (at least to some degree) the burden of proof to those who claim that controlling for "all" interfering variables would plunge the rate of payoff to education to unfavorable levels.[18]

A second popular attack concedes the differential ability issue, but questions whether the higher incomes of the better educated represent a net gain for the community. Graduating from high school or college may mean much higher lifetime incomes even for the sort of people who usually terminate earlier; but—so the critique runs—that merely implies that employers have a preference for degree holders that, in turn, may be founded largely on a belief that graduates have demonstrated desirable ambition and persistence by the successful completion of a long course of study. If the graduates had not been available, nongraduates might have been hired at roughly the same rate of pay and have performed on the job at roughly the same level of efficiency. Thus, while the individual may find a diploma useful in the scramble for high paying jobs, his gain may entail a commensurate loss for someone else. And, as a corollary, it could be argued that the individual who escapes poverty by an education route may, in the process, "bump" a fellow worker into the poverty category.

---

[18] James Morgan and Martin David ("Education and Income," *Quarterly Journal of Economics*, Vol. 77, No. 3 [August 1963], pp. 423-37) demonstrate that if one adopts sufficiently harsh assumptions, returns can be pushed close to zero for some educational increments. Their assumptions and controls, however, are overly severe. In multiple regressions performed on their sample survey of workers, at least two of the variables controlled for—supervisory responsibility and attitude of the respondent to achievement—very likely picked up some effects of education that are natural concomitants of greater productivity and income. But even more influential than "overcontrol" is their use of differences in full-time earnings associated with different educational attainments as the basis for estimating returns, rather than the more orthodox procedure of using yearly earnings unadjusted for employment. The studies cited in note 12 all considered the reduction of time unemployed, and the consequent increase in lifetime earnings, as part of the benefit from education. Morgan and David do not, though they concede that "some unemployment might be directly attributable to the lack of flexibility and foresight associated with less formal education" (*ibid.*, p. 436). The handling of differential unemployment rates is discussed in Chap. 3, pp. 42-49.

But those who drop out in the middle of high school or college succeed in earning appreciably more than those who never started, thus implying that something more than the magic of the diploma attracts employers.[19] It could, of course, be argued that employers are impressed even by an unsuccessful effort to obtain a diploma. Conversely, however, they might be repelled by the apparent tendency of the prospective employee to start a project and then not finish it.

Moreover, there is a positive relationship between the measured amount learned by individuals completing the *same* level of schooling and their income during their working years.[20] This suggests that the absorption of learning is economically rewarding in and of itself. Though it might be argued that employers are dazzled by high grades when selecting employees, it is interesting to note that the observed income differential between low scoring and high scoring students was recorded several years after (and in most cases over a decade after) the termination of schooling. It would seem more reasonable to believe that demonstrated competence on the job rather than a lingering reputation as a good student with good grades led to this differential.

Finally, there is a large gap between actual economic growth of the American economy and the growth that can be explained by

[19] In the studies cited in note 12, p. 8, the rate of return for completing only two years of high school was found to be nearly as high as that for completing high school, the rate for completing only "some" college below 10 percent though above 5 percent, and the rate on four years of college in the neighborhood of 12 percent. This difference may be attributed to the prestige of the degree, but it may just as easily be explained as an indivisibility phenomenon: the learning acquired at the beginning of college may be rendered much more useful if complemented by more specialized courses in the later years.

[20] See in particular Dael Wolfle and J. Smith, "The Occupational Value of Education for Superior High School Graduates," *Journal of Higher Education* (April 1956), pp. 201-13; and Donald S. Bridgman, "Success in College and Business," *Personnel Journal*, Vol. 9 (June 1930), pp. 1-18. Both focus on the relationship between class standing and later income. Preliminary results of a study relating the scores of servicemen on the Armed Forces Qualifying Test, years of school completed, and income as recorded in Social Security records indicate a stronger partial correlation between test scores and later-life income than between school years and later-life income. See Phillips Cutright, "A Pilot Study of Factors in Economic Success and Failure Based on Selective Service and Social Security Records," Social Security Administration, 1964 (mimeo).

the measured increases in physical capital and in the size of the labor force. If it is insisted that education does little in improving the actual efficiency of workers, one is hard pressed to account for the size of this gap.[21] One would have to assign an implausibly large amount of credit to technological change.

Though none of these arguments is absolutely clinching, together they succeed in strengthening the link between education and productivity; and with this link more secure, it becomes harder to claim that the income gain experienced by an educated individual simply comes at the expense of someone else. This does not mean that the entire income gain observed is a net social gain, but it does imply a large part of it probably is.

To sum up, the present state of empirical knowledge suggests that the forces tending to produce underinvestment in education are stronger than the countervailing force of current government subsidization. While it is true that the payoff rate evidence noted here does not relate specifically to the people in poverty, it would nevertheless seem to apply a fortiori to this group. It is the poor, after all, who are likely to have the most difficulty in getting around capital market imperfections and the other problems associated with the fact that education is an embodied investment. Moreover, the existence of exceptionally high rates of payoff for lower levels of schooling also suggests that underinvestment in education is a problem closely associated with poverty: it is the children of the poor who most often leave school early, and it is the earliest school leavers who have the highest odds for earning poverty level incomes.

It should again be noted that the above line of argument does not take account of the social benefits of education or the nonfinancial returns to the individual. These will be considered in Chapter 6. However, given the focus of the present study on the relation between poverty and education, our primary concern will continue to be with the personal income impact of education.

[21] For a recent discussion, see Edward F. Denison, "Measuring the Contribution of Education (and the Residual) to Economic Growth," plus comments and rejoinder, in *The Residual Factor and Economic Growth* (Paris: Organization for Economic Cooperation and Development, 1964), pp. 13-100.

Current Federal Policy

A disquieting feature of the evidence on the rate of return to education is its oblique, and thus uncertain, relationship to contemporary policy. Current federal education programs attempt to help the poor to continue their formal schooling, but the primary emphasis nevertheless lies in two other directions. One direction is the establishment of special types of training outside the regular school system: preschool classes in the form of Operation Headstart, and vocationally oriented training through programs like Job Corps and Neighborhood Youth Corps. The second major approach, the aim of Title I of the Elementary and Secondary Education Act of 1965, involves increasing the quality of formal education for poor children at both primary and high school levels.[22]

This is not to say that the continuation of formal schooling is not anticipated as a result of these programs. Indeed, one of the stated motives of the Neighborhood Youth Corps is the encouragement of school continuation. It works toward this end by providing part-time subsidized work for students who feel financial pressures to quit school and by counseling and training dropouts (and potential dropouts) in the hope that they will perceive more clearly the connection between learning and future income, thus inducing them to return to (or remain in) high school. Similarly, the preschool programs and the improved quality of education in the regular school years should, to some extent, induce a higher proportion of pupils to stay in school longer. But, despite these aims and expectations, there is little question that the current antipoverty efforts are founded on a belief that simple prolongation of schooling, of present quality, is of secondary importance.

Good reasons can be given for this belief. On an optimistic note, one might argue that, while encouraging youths to continue school has a respectable payoff rate, the current education programs should result in even larger economic gains for the poor per dollar spent.

---

[22] For a concise description of the federal education efforts relating to poverty, see *Economic Report of the President, January 1966, Together with the Annual Report of the Council of Economic Advisers,* pp. 94-100.

In defense of preschool training, one might cite the recently accumulated evidence that critical habits of learning are acquired in the preschool years, implying that additional schooling time at the beginning may be the most efficacious way to lengthen the duration of education.[23] Job-oriented training too is a form of extra schooling, and since it is geared specifically to the development of marketable skills, it could be argued that it should have at least as much economic effectiveness as a commensurate amount of general education. Finally, increasing the quality of schooling and (presumably) increasing the amount learned in the same period of time have the economic appeal of entailing no extra costs in the form of foregone income.

Another, less cheerful, point of view begins with the presumption that schools servicing a decidedly underprivileged clientele are, for various reasons, seriously ineffective in their current mode of operation.[24] Thus, while encouraging an "ordinary" potential dropout to continue formal schooling might be a good idea, the slum school dropout may be missing out on very little by his early departure. Moreover, even if continuation would be economically advantageous to the slum school youth, it might be argued that the school has typically performed such a poor job of winning the trust of the pupil that a large and expensive effort is required to persuade him of this advantage. If slum schools appear deficient enough to raise these sorts of speculations, one might well turn to educational programs outside the regular school system and attempt simultaneously to do as much as possible about reforming and improving the quality of instruction in public schools.

Regardless of the reasoning behind the current legislation—and there will be no attempt here to judge which points of view are most prominent and most persuasive—the fact remains that the impact of the educational changes recently put into effect is not the kind of impact or change measured by the payoff-rate evidence discussed in the immediately preceding section. New measurements are needed that have a more direct bearing on current policy.

[23] Benjamin S. Bloom, *Stability and Change in Human Characteristics* (Wiley, 1964), has been especially influential in directing attention to the preschool years.
[24] Two well-documented accounts with this point of view are HARYOU (Harlem Youth Opportunities Unlimited), *Youth in the Ghetto* (HARYOU, 1964); and James B. Conant, *Slums and Suburbs* (McGraw-Hill, 1961).

Unfortunately, hard data on the outcomes of the recently inaugurated programs have not yet appeared. At present, there are available only a handful of case studies—all predating the antipoverty legislation—that give any clue as to whether these special types of educational change have high or low payoff rates. Chapters 3, 4, and 5 attempt to build upon these studies and add some new observations that are even more specifically related to the kinds of education programs involved in the new legislation. They compute a series of comparable benefit-cost estimates in the hope of allowing a judgment about which types of programs are most efficient in raising the incomes of the poor and whether the efficiency of particular types of programs is sufficiently high to warrant continuation or expansion. Since the number of case studies is few, the results are necessarily tentative and preliminary. But the methodology developed will be applicable as more data become available, thus permitting firmer conclusions in the future. The reader may, therefore, choose to treat the "early results" as the flesh and blood illustrations for the methodological approach and as suggestive of the needed directions for future research.

The computations of Chapters 3, 4, and 5 are made with the help of some simplifying assumptions. Chapter 6 questions and tries to improve upon some of these assumptions. The issues treated there include the intergenerational transmission of education, the effect on payoff rates of large "supramarginal" changes in educational expenditures, and the question of benefits from education other than direct money income gain.

Before tackling these subjects it is necessary to look more carefully at the benefit-cost criterion of dollar gains contrasted to dollar costs. In much of the current discussion of the poverty program, the commonly accepted measure of "success" is the raising of individual incomes to a target level called a "poverty line." For several reasons, this criterion may not yield the same policy conclusions as a straight comparison of dollar income gains with dollar costs. Thus, another apparent dissonance occurs between the payoff-rate evidence discussed above and the question of current policy choice. The theoretical basis for a poverty line, its implication for policy, and its integration with orthodox benefit-cost notions are the subjects of Chapter 2.

CHAPTER II

Poverty Lines and the Criteria of Policy Choice

With few exceptions, economists who address themselves to the poverty issue devote a major part of their effort to defining, clarifying, and utilizing the idea that there is an income level that separates poor people from nonpoor people. Such an income level implies that bringing any individual above that level solves the "poverty problem" for that individual. It would appear to follow that once everyone is brought above that line, complete victory will have been achieved in the war on poverty.

Integrating this idea with the technique of benefit-cost analysis is the most important task of this chapter. A number of steps are involved. For didactic purposes, the first step is to distill the wide range of policy options into simple, but still meaningful, alternatives. Next comes a critical analysis of how the poverty line, in its currently accepted form, serves as a basis for policy choice. It is argued that the conceptual shortcomings of this basis make necessary a reformulation of the poverty line notion. The upshot is the construction of two poverty lines which, in turn, could be used as "guideposts" for weighting dollar benefits according to specified ranges of family income.

The analysis depends upon a definition of poverty as an economic condition. Thus its "cure" involves raising the incomes of the poor. Were poverty defined as a "culture," as a set of attitudes, increases in income would not in themselves be sufficient to guarantee the elimination of poverty (unless the change in income resulted in changes in "culture"). Though the economic definition may be a narrow one, it is surely a major part of any definition and may be considerd a basic guide to public policy.

Alternative Antipoverty Devices

The criteria discussed and developed in this chapter are aimed at discovering the optimum role of education in a war on poverty. Other forms of antipoverty action are not evaluated here. Occasionally, when it is necessary to compare alternatives, the analysis relies on a simplified choice between education and direct transfer payments. Education is treated as unadulterated human investment that affects nothing other than the productive capacity and income of the persons directly experiencing the education. Transfers are thought of as money payments with no strings attached, and as having no secondary repercussions on the amount or quality of work performed by the persons receiving the payments.

Characterizing antipoverty alternatives as a choice between education and income transfers is not uncommon. Several observers have viewed the balancing of these approaches as basic and also very difficult,[1] and others have strongly advocated either education or transfers as the "proper" keystone in a war on poverty.[2] The ex-

---

[1] George H. Hildebrand, in "The Economics of Poverty" (session of the 1964 meeting of the American Economic Association), *American Economic Review*, Vol. 55, No. 2 (May 1965), pp. 541-43; and John T. Dunlop, "Poverty: Definition and Measurement," in Chamber of Commerce of the U.S.A., Task Force on Economic Growth and Opportunity, *The Concept of Poverty* (1965), pp. 95-111.

[2] Strongly worded statements in favor of education can be found in Committee for Economic Development (CED), *Raising Low Incomes Through Improved Education* (CED, 1965); and in the speech by Walter Heller at the Annual Public Affairs Forum, Indiana State College, reprinted in *American Poverty: Its Causes and Cures* (Indiana, Pa.: Indiana State College, 1965). Advocacy of transfers can be found in Harry Johnson, in "The Economics of Poverty," *American Economic Review*, Vol. 55, No. 2 (May 1965), pp. 543-45; and in Milton Friedman, *Capitalism and Freedom* (University of Chicago Press, 1962), pp. 190-95. One could treat education and transfers as complements, favorably reinforcing one another. Thus, a poor child might be able

isting and proposed legislation aimed at poverty is composed mainly of human investment programs and direct transfers of money or consumption goods. All of the human investment is not education, nor is all of the direct help in the form of simple transfer payments; moreover, it is difficult to identify any program as a pure case of either form of antipoverty action. Nevertheless, an analysis in terms of pure alternatives will shed some light on the mixed and complex cases.

Problems of a Poverty Line

If poverty is defined by an income level, and the number of people who cross the line is the gauge of how successfully the poverty problem is being solved, alternative antipoverty policies should be evaluated in terms of the (predicted) number of people moved across the line. General policy discussions nearly always employ this standard.[3] And the few attempts to judge alternative policy approaches empirically have given serious attention to this criterion only. Although the empirical studies focus on the antipoverty effect of stimulating growth and lowering unemployment, the education-versus-transfer choice does receive some comment, and the line-crossing standard is applied in this instance as well.[4]

---

to take much better advantage of improved schooling if, at the same time, income transfers to his parents made life more comfortable at home. This possibility does not reduce the need for specifying the optimum mix between transfers and education; it only makes the chore more complicated. Chapter 6 comments further on this.

[3] See, for instance, *Economic Report of the President, January 1964, Together with the Annual Report of the Council of Economic Advisers* (1964), p. 58.

[4] Lowell E. Gallaway, "The Foundations of the 'War on Poverty,'" *American Economic Review*, Vol. 55, No. 1 (March 1965), pp. 122-30; and W. H. Locke Anderson, "Trickling Down: The Relationship Between Economic Growth and the Extent of Poverty Among American Families," *Quarterly Journal of Economics*, Vol. 68, No. 4 (November 1964), pp. 511-24. Gallaway, the more explicit on human investment versus transfers, forecasts that, if the economy grows as expected, only 6 percent of all families will have less than $3,000 incomes in 1980. He contrasts this 6 percent figure with the allegedly faulty 10 percent prediction of the Council of Economic Advisers and concludes that human investment is a clumsy weapon for moving this relatively small group above the line. "Direct-subsidy" programs are suggested as an alternative (see especially p. 130).

Does the line-crossing criterion, by itself, provide a satisfactory picture of antipoverty accomplishments? It would seem not, for substantial movements *within* the poverty category may be ignored. Thus, though a given policy could push a large number of families across the line, the crossings may occur mainly among those on the verge of escaping poverty and have little effect on people at the very bottom of the income distribution. An alternative action may do a great deal for the bottom group, moving many families, say, from a $1,000 to a $2,500 income. In this case, counting only those who cross the line might be a vast underestimate of the true relief of poverty. Surely a $1,000 to $2,500 improvement is at least as important an achievement as moving from a $2,500 to a $3,001 income position.

This flaw in the simple poverty line measure is the apparent reason for Robert Lampman's suggestion of a second dimension, the "poverty income gap," which is defined as the "aggregate amount by which the present poor population's income falls below $3,000 per family or $1,500 per unrelated individual."[5] This measure is the sum of the difference between family (or individual) income and the poverty line for all families (or individuals) in the poverty category. The poverty line notion is not thereby abandoned; it is simply used in a slightly different way in order to correct the most obvious shortcoming of the line-crossing measure. According to Lampman, "it helps to think of the goal in two parts: the reduction of the poverty rate [that is, line crossings] and the reduction of the poverty income gap."[6]

While this double goal takes into account the income gains short of the line, it introduces the problem of how to balance the two goals when making a final decision.[7] And, more importantly, income gains *above* the line are still treated arbitrarily. Moving a

---

[5] Robert J. Lampman, "Approaches to the Reduction of Poverty," *American Economic Review*, Vol. 55, No. 2 (May 1965), p. 523.

[6] *Ibid.*

[7] Lampman argues that "we want to work from the top down and from the bottom up so to speak. The aim of policy should be to do each type of reduction without slowing the other . . ." (*ibid.*, pp. 523-24). This neglects the possibility of a budget constraint forcing a choice between alternative policies, one of which essentially does a "bottom up" job and the other especially well at getting people across the $3,000 line (the "top-down" approach).

family from a $2,500 to a $4,000 income achieves the same (for both goals) as a move from a $2,500 to $3,001 income. Thus, no distinction is made between "barely" above and "comfortably" above the poverty line. Do we really wish to hide this distinction?

Strict adherence to the Lampman criteria implies a peculiar "kink" in social preferences. The measure of the poverty income gap counts income gains just above the line at zero value (as regards the antipoverty goal), but gains just below the line, as well as gains far below the line, at full dollar value. This procedure suggests that the added social utility of all incremental dollar improvements is stable over the entire range below $3,000 and then plummets as soon as the $3,000 mark is reached. It is unlikely that this adequately describes either collective or individual preference functions.

In practice, the Lampman double rule of thumb, or even the simple line-crossing measure, may frequently give the same answers as would the most theoretically appealing set of criteria. In decisions concerning the relative emphasis of education in an antipoverty effort, however, the Lampman criteria may often be inadequate.

Improved education for children from poor families is aimed at rescuing individuals from future adult poverty. It cannot be assumed that each case is successful. Nor should it be assumed that without this extra educational thrust all the children will end up as poor adults. It follows that education, as compared to income transfers or income in kind, lacks "precision" as a poverty weapon. Dollar transfers can presumably be focused on persons in poverty. Dollar gains from education are more diffused. We must simply treat the youths we *think* will turn out poor; though we might be able to predict the percentage of a certain type of youth who will end up poor, it is difficult to isolate the sure bets. Some of the income gains from education will therefore involve moving future adults from future nonpoor levels of income to still higher nonpoor levels. Thus, only a fraction of the total educational expenditure will contribute to the specified goals in the Lampman criteria.

To illustrate this quantitatively, we can estimate the spread of future income positions among a set of youths apparently destined for a high incidence of poverty. We can estimate this from the current earnings of young high school dropouts. From the earnings of high school graduates, we also can estimate what their incomes would look like if we improved their education.

Table 1 shows the expected distribution of earnings by dollar categories among representative groups of dropouts and high school graduates. It reveals that a young dropout does not inevitably earn less than $3,000 per year and that graduation hardly assures earnings greater than $3,000. Even so, the graduate enjoys an average income $487 higher than the dropout. What does this configuration imply for the Lampman criteria and the choice between education and transfers?

To derive an uncomplex answer to this question, let us suppose an education program could be applied to the 1,000 dropouts which converts them instantaneously into 1,000 graduates. Suppose also that the gains from education are *all concentrated in a single year* so that the configuration of yearly incomes in Table 1 summarizes the *whole* of the gain.[8] Under these assumptions, the number of individuals who can be expected to rise above the $3,000 mark (the first half of the Lampman test) is shown in the third line of Table 1. Adding the differences in the number of individuals appearing in the three lowest earnings categories indicates that the education program should pull 116 individuals across the $3,000 line. The results on the other half of the Lampman test can be estimated by multiplying each of these three differences times the relevant dollar distance below the $3,000 line and then adding the separate products. Thus, if we assume that this dollar distance is represented by the class marks of the respective earnings categories, $2,500 can be multiplied by 96, etc., yielding a total of $268,000.

This indicates that the poverty income gap would be reduced by $268,000, which in turn implies that the education would not be an efficient means of reducing the gap unless it cost less than $268,000. If education costs were in excess of this figure, it follows that a transfer program, costing the same amount as the education program, could succeed in eliminating a greater amount of the

---

[8] These severe assumptions are only in the interest of simplicity. Dealing with gains strung out over a long period of time would not change the nature of our result but would lead to considerable complexity.

TABLE 1

Expected Distribution of Yearly Earnings for 1,000 High School Graduates and 1,000 High School Dropouts[a]

Educational Level	Mean Earnings	Number Earning											
		$1 to $999	$1,000 to $1,999	$2,000 to $2,999	$3,000 to $3,999	$4,000 to $4,999	$5,000 to $5,999	$6,000 to $6,999	$7,000 to $9,999	$10,000 to $14,999	$15,000 to $24,999	$25,000 and Over
High school graduate	$3,036	165	170	178	192	153	87	32	18	3	1	1
High school dropout	$2,549	261	188	180	162	111	61	22	12	2	1	0
Difference	$ 487	−96	−18	−2	30	42	26	10	6	1	0	1

[a] Calculated from data on the earned income of males between 18 and 24 years of age in the experienced civilian labor force, as recorded in U.S. Department of Commerce, Bureau of the Census, U.S. Census of Population: 1960, Occupation by Earnings and Education, PC(2)-7B (1963), Table 4, p. 244.

poverty income gap. In this circumstance, it is also apparent that transfers could easily bring more individuals across the $3,000 line than could education.

It is interesting to contrast this result with the answer provided by benefit-cost analysis, comparing average income gains and average costs, or—what amounts to the same thing—total income gains and total costs. In the example at hand, the average dropout gains $487 annually, and total income gains for the education program are thus $487,000 per year. If costs did turn out to be $268,000, this would yield a benefit-cost ratio of 1.7, indicating that total returns were 70 percent higher than costs. This appears to be a very handsome payoff rate. Yet, according to the poverty income gap measure, costs of $268,000 would imply that we are on the borderline of indifference between adopting and rejecting the education program. Benefit-cost analysis would suggest that the education program must cost more than $487,000 if we are to reject it in preference for direct help. The reasons for this difference are clear: in one case we count all income gains, in the other only the gains in the poverty area. The "output" measures differ, and it is obvious that the choice of measures is an important task. As indicated earlier, in a poverty-oriented program the criteria of success may well place greater emphasis on the poor than on those above the poverty line. Yet it is clear that gains above the line must be valued at more than zero.

One might therefore argue that a straightforward comparison of total income gains with total costs is a more reasonable standard for policy choice. But this standard raises problems also. Theoretical welfare economics has long preached concern not only for the average level but also for the distribution of benefits, and recent essays on benefit-cost techniques have stressed the same point.[9] In allocating an antipoverty budget, this advice cannot be easily ignored. To take the extreme case, it is surely inappropriate to

[9] Arthur Maass, "Benefit-Cost Analysis: Its Relevance to Public Investment Decisions," *Quarterly Journal of Economics*, Vol. 80, No. 2 (May 1966), pp. 208-26; and Burton A. Weisbrod, "Income Redistribution Effects and Benefit–Cost Analysis," in Samuel B. Chase, Jr. (ed.), *Problems in Public Expenditure Analysis* (Brookings Institution, 1968), pp. 177-222.

"squander" a budget set aside for poverty alleviation on programs that help only a relatively small number of presently poor individuals reach exceedingly high levels of income.

This issue undoubtedly has numerous resolutions. The one suggested below is relatively simple. It manages to synthesize several widely held points of view, and it appears to solve more problems than it begets.

Dual Poverty Lines

Clearly, the way in which we measure the effectiveness of an antipoverty program depends heavily on the way we define poverty. Contemporary writers appear to agree that the idea of a poverty line cannot be abandoned and that the line cannot be put in absolute terms, but must heavily involve "cultural factors" and the overall level of material well-being. There is considerable *dis*agreement (among experts and laymen alike) about exactly where the line should be drawn.[10]

The poverty line that is used for public policy decisions is a product of social consensus. The conceptual anomalies encountered in the last section hint, however, that a single line does not adequately summarize our true social intent. If we wish to discover the nature of social preferences, we must examine the shape —if not the exact quantitative values—of individual preferences.

To do this, it helps to resort to the fiction of a representative "economic man" concerned about social goals, and in particular the social goal of poverty alleviation.[11]

What should a socially conscious citizen keep in mind when he tries to decide for himself where he would like a poverty line to

[10] For a review of recent commentary on poverty lines, see App. A. It indicates, among other things, that there is considerable semantic and epistemological confusion on the issue. An important side purpose of this chapter (and the appendix) is to attempt to iron out this confusion. Thus we must probe a little more deeply into definitional matters than would be necessary simply to derive sensible criteria.

[11] For convenience, this discussion focuses on a representative citizen not in poverty. The analysis can be applied (with slight modification) to the socially conscious poor person as well; App. A discusses this further.

be? To answer this question, we must first ask why the citizen is interested in poverty in the first place. And the answer to this would seem to be that poverty is a phenomenon he wishes did not exist; that is, the presence of poverty causes him displeasure. If this is the case, our citizen should try to specify where that displeasure begins. In trying to determine where a poverty line should be, he must decide what is the *highest* standard of living still low enough to arouse his social concern and altruistic sympathies.

Here it might be argued that a genuinely altruistic person would have no limitation. Any degree of material want, experienced by any person, might cause him displeasure; and he would, for instance, be willing to make some personal sacrifice to see a very wealthy man fulfill his lifelong wish of acquiring a second yacht. That, however, would seem to be an extremely rare attitude. And, while not challenging the existence of such attitudes, it is assumed that our socially conscious citizen does have an upper limit to his altruistic sentiments as these relate to material want; which is to say, there is some income level above which he feels no particular social obligation to a fellow citizen and is not inclined to make any meaningful sacrifice to see him rise still higher.[12]

Deciding upon this income level would amount to the establishment of one poverty line. Perhaps the best way to interpret this line is to say that income gains by any person below this line would provide our representative individual a positive external benefit for which he would exchange some amount of money. Income gains by individuals exactly at the line or above it would, on the other hand, provide him no vicarious pleasure, and no finite amounts of money would be exchanged for such improvements.

But this line only specifies the number of "units" of poverty our citizen *might* be willing to have bought into nonpoverty. Since he must pay part of the bill through taxes, it is likely he would *not* recommend that *all* those below the line be brought up to exactly that income level. Bringing all poor individuals above the poverty

---

[12] One might also imagine an individual who feels absolutely no displeasure from witnessing his fellow citizens experiencing material deprivation, regardless of how extreme that deprivation might be. Quite likely, he is not so rare as the "undiscriminating" altruist who has no upper limit. Individuals having no empathetic concern would, it seems, have no interest in poverty lines except to say that they categorically oppose the whole idea.

line as determined above would imply that the "public good" of poverty elimination was being purchased up to the point of complete satiety.[13] Since few goods, public or private, are consumed to the point of satiety, a second line is needed to define the income level that, *at the going cost of antipoverty programs,* our representative citizen is indifferent about altering upwards.

Suppose that $1 gained by the individuals in poverty costs $1 of poverty assistance (and of tax money) under either a straight income-transfer or a human investment program. Suppose also that the cost is the same for helping all individuals below the first poverty line. In other words, the income of any poor person can be raised by $1 (no more or less) if it is agreed that $1 more of taxes should be collected in behalf of poverty. If there were in fact a referendum on this issue, a logical decision by our representative citizen would involve weighing the extra dollar's worth of antipoverty action against the share of the new expense he must pay. So far, the individual's decision process is more or less parallel with what must be thought about in the standard case of "public goods."[14] But poverty, as defined by our first poverty line, is necessarily a heteroge-

[13] The orthodox theory of "public goods" seeks to answer the question "how many units of the commodity or service in question should be purchased by tax-paying citizens." The solution we are about to suggest here provides the same sort of answer. See Richard A. Musgrave, *The Theory of Public Finance* (McGraw-Hill, 1959), pp. 73-84; and Paul A. Samuelson, "Diagrammatic Exposition of a Theory of Public Expenditures," *Review of Economics and Statistics,* Vol. 37, No. 4 (November 1955), pp. 350-56. The general advice given by this theory is that purchases of additional units of a public commodity should cease when the marginal utility of private expenditures relinquished equals that of the public commodity. The advice is a direct extension of the theory of private consumption. The difference is that preferences cannot be revealed by market behavior but must instead be manifested by some sort of electoral process. See App. A for more detailed discussion of poverty alleviation as a public good.

[14] The Musgrave and Samuelson versions of the theory of public goods (as well as many earlier versions) attempt to determine tax shares simultaneously with the specification of the optimum number of units to be purchased. (Musgrave, *The Theory of Public Finance,* p. 80; Samuelson, "Diagrammatic Exposition of a Theory of Public Expenditures," p. 255.) But this leads to exceedingly complex problems, regardless of what public good is in question. Hence, to keep the analysis relatively uncluttered, it is here assumed that the tax share question has been settled and that our citizen knows exactly how much of the new burden he will shoulder if the (hypothetical) referendum passes. Further comment on this appears in App. A.

It is reasonable to think that poor individuals who expect to make a net gain in disposable income from a poverty program would always be in favor of a larger, and

neous commodity. It is reasonable to suppose therefore that the typical citizen who is indifferent about his affluent neighbors' income gains but happy about gains enjoyed by the relatively unaffluent also feels more strongly about a dollar's worth of help for the abysmally poor than for those who are only very poor.

This heterogeneity permits establishment of a second poverty line, for it implies that the typical citizen should reach his final decision by steps. First, he should ask himself whether he wants to contribute the requisite amount to bring the abysmally poor to the next higher level of income; next, whether he wants to bring this second category to the third plateau; and so on, one step at a time. An affirmative answer for the step in question means that our citizen wishes no one to have an income below this level and that he is willing to share his (predetermined) part of the burden in making this an actuality. The point at which he calls a halt can be summed up in a second poverty line, which obviously must lie below the first.

This derivation preserves the notion of poverty lines and, at the same time, recognizes different degrees of poverty and does not contain any suggestion of a kink in preference functions.[15] It also reinterprets the worry that complete elimination of poverty is never attainable, suggesting that one-hundred-percent eradication amounts to consuming poverty reduction to the point of satiety. While this may not ever quite occur, the passage of time and the growth in per capita income may nevertheless bring us quite close, since greater overall affluence suggests that we can afford to spend more on poverty alleviation. But rising income levels may also incline us to set higher standards as well—in other words, to raise the "top" poverty line. Progress toward the eradication of poverty can thus be visualized as the bottom line pursuing the top poverty line over time.

This derivation also makes clear that relative prices should help

---

still larger, program. Nevertheless, it is possible to inquire how much pleasure (if any) they would experience from seeing *other* poor people grow less poor. It might be noted that a similar theoretical separation is required in the more standard "public goods" case. See App. A.

[15] Others have also suggested two poverty lines, but without an explicit theoretical mechanism behind either line and without the same implications of the lines derived above. See App. A.

determine the degree to which we reduce poverty. If the ratio of tax costs to antipoverty benefits changes, so would the level of the bottom line. Thus, if payoff ratios for improved education are discovered to be considerably greater than one-to-one, the price of poverty elimination is reduced and more "units" should be purchased. This can be represented by a simple upward shift in our bottom poverty line. As more efficient devices are found, poverty elimination becomes less expensive; and, if it is cheap enough, we might consume this service close to the point of satiety.[16]

It must be remembered, however, that even though education may have a high average payoff rate, returns for individuals are widely dispersed. While our model does not contain sharply kinked preferences (which, as we witnessed, heavily burdened the argument for education), it nevertheless assumes that we have greater relative concern for more severe levels of poverty. It follows that transfers will have some advantage when it comes to pinpointing our efforts. Taking this into account—and assuming that poverty is defined as an economic condition and not as a "culture" —what does our model imply for the choice between education and transfers?

Weighting Gains Between the Poverty Lines

If two poverty lines are established to reflect a social consensus of people reasoning in the above fashion, they form guideposts for weighting dollar gains experienced by the poor in various income ranges. Since those above the top line are no longer considered in poverty, the dollar gains at that level and above should be counted at zero weight. In the range immediately under this line, gains should obviously be counted at close to zero weight. To get some

[16] Some authors have expressed puzzlement over why a war on poverty has been launched at this particular moment in history. While many social and political causes have been mentioned, a convincing economic rationale has not been put forward. The possible role of changing relative prices has not been advanced as an explanation. In this connection, it is interesting to note that the empirical evidence on the high rate of return to education appeared not too long before the start of the war on poverty.

idea of how to "shade" the weights below the top line, we need to draw an additional inference from the bottom line.

The required inference, implicit in the above derivation, is that the bottom poverty line describes the point where taxpayers are willing to give up one dollar—no more, no less—to see poor people in this particular income range benefit by one dollar. Thus, gains near the bottom poverty line should be weighted by approximately full value. Gains between the bottom and top poverty lines can then be graduated between one and zero, and gains below the bottom line weighted at greater than one. With these weights established, comparisons between competing antipoverty programs can proceed in a more reasonable and equitable fashion.

Consider the earlier example involving high school dropouts. Suppose a $3,000 income formed the lower poverty line and a $5,000 income the upper line. Since this implies an obligation to bring everyone below $3,000 up to that line, the phrasing of the decision on education should go as follows: should some of the money planned for transfers be put into education instead? In other words, the total bill implied by the first poverty line can be made to serve as an "interim" budget constraint, and the mix of education and transfers can be determined by evaluating the effects of shifting chunks of the budget into education.

In the earlier example the "instant education" of 1,000 dropouts resulted in $268,000 worth of income gains occurring in the critical range below $3,000. (See Table 1 and accompanying discussion in the text.) Rather than speaking of this as a reduction of the poverty income gap, the present framework suggests that $268,000 be thought of as that portion of the former transfer obligation that is successfully met by the alternative of education. If the costs of the education are less than $268,000, it is clear that the education should be undertaken. But, unlike our earlier example involving only one poverty line, costs can be somewhat in excess of $268,000 and education still appear an advisable form of antipoverty action.

Thinking in terms of an interim budget (which, via transfers, brings all 1,000 dropouts up to a $3,000 level) it follows that if the educational program costs more than $268,000 (and is undertaken anyway), then the minimum income enjoyed by this group of

1,000 must slip below the $3,000 mark unless additional tax money is raised. To find out whether we are willing to let this minimum level slip—or, alternatively, whether we are willing to raise the extra funds to maintain it—we must evaluate the income gains that occur between $3,000 and $5,000.

Assuming that all dollar gains above $5,000 count for zero, a linear weighting would imply that gains in the $3,000-$4,000 range should be multiplied by 0.67 and gains in the $4,000-$5,000 range by 0.33. To count the extra dollar gains from education, the 116 dropouts who rise above the $3,000 mark can be grouped into three categories according to the positive differences that appear in the third line of Table 1. The three categories are: (a) the 321 individuals who end up in the $3,000-$4,000 range; (b) the 40 who climb to the $4,000-$5,000 range; and (c) the 44 who surpass the $5,000 mark. The first two groups can be evaluated by their class marks. Thus, each member of group (a) can be said to be $500 better off than if the entire budget had been used for transfers, and this gain can be multiplied by 0.67 for each individual in this category. Similarly, each member of group (b) is $1,500 better off, and the first $1,000 can be multiplied by 0.67 and the last $500 by 0.33. Group (c) gains $1,000 in each of the two relevant ranges, and the first $1,000 can be weighted by 0.67 and the second by 0.33.

Under this procedure, the total gains above the $3,000 mark would be evaluated at $88,510. Adding this to the $268,000 worth of transfer payments that are no longer needed suggests that the education could cost as much as $356,500 and still be an advisable course of antipoverty action.[17]

While these assumptions and procedures entail a less stringent

[17] This is a slight overestimate. If costs were indeed $356,000, this means that all those still below the $3,000 mark would receive, collectively, $88,510 less in the way of transfers should the total budget not be revised. Under our assumptions, the education would leave 513 below this mark (that is, the total number of individuals in the three lowest income categories in the first line of Table 1). Presuming an evenly spread cut in transfers, each person in this group would receive $173 less. This loss must be weighted by exactly one if we are to say it is exactly balanced by the $88,510 worth of weighted gains accrued in the $3,000-$5,000 range. The relatively small amount lost by each individual suggests that a weighting of one is not unreasonable. But a strictly continuous weighting scale, plus the demands of logical consistency, suggests that this loss be weighted by something a little more than one.

test for education than does the Lampman double rule of thumb, this criterion clearly is more stringent than a straightforward comparison of unweighted dollar benefits and costs. As a gauge of how much more so, we might note what unweighted benefit-cost ratio coincides with the break-even point as determined by our weighted income criteria. With the given magnitude and distribution of income gains in the above example, the break-even point would occur when the total cost of education stands at $356,510. The total unweighted income gain, it will be recalled, amounted to $487,000 (the per-individual gain multiplied by 1,000). The unweighted benefit-cost ratio thus equals 1.37 when the criteria based on the two poverty lines state that we should be indifferent between educating the dropouts and not educating them.

Demands of the Dual Poverty Line Technique

Reasoning through the problem of poverty from the viewpoint of an individual citizen leads almost unavoidably to the conclusion that two poverty lines, rather than one, should be established. This manner of reasoning makes clear, at the same time, that poverty lines need not imply any discontinuity in preferences. Among the implications of this approach is a reinterpretation of what is meant by a total victory against poverty. And, most importantly, it is suggested that the goal of poverty elimination and the technique of benefit-cost analysis can be reasonably harmonized by the graduated weighting of income gains, which in turn follows directly from the establishment of the two poverty lines. Further implications of the analysis are best postponed until we encounter specific conceptual problems requiring resolution.

The resulting procedure for choosing between antipoverty policies is not problem free. First of all, the data requirements are quite severe. We not only have to know the average return from a given type of human investment, but also details about its variance. This, however, is true for even the simplest "line crossing" standard of antipoverty success; and, if enough is known about the variance of returns to predict how many poor people will cross some poverty threshold, it is likely that enough is also known to compute a weighted benefit-cost estimate as well. Second, it is sensible to think that poverty lines will shift (probably upward) through time, so that the calculation of benefits will in fact be much more complicated than the simple example above suggests. But this problem is also present in a single poverty line system, providing that it is recognized that poverty is a question of social consensus. Third, the model developed above cannot be interpreted as a simple mandate to bring all those below a certain line precisely up to it. To avoid interfering unduly with work incentives, some graduation in the final distribution of transfers is surely called for. Judging the appropriate degree of graduation is always a difficult problem, and the analysis above makes little contribution to its solution.

Finally, there is the question of whether we really want to weight some dollar gains at values less than one. It can be argued quite reasonably that other aims of social policy are advanced by any net gain in income and that counting income gains from antipoverty education at zero value is not justifiable. If, however, high social priority has been given to poverty alleviation, but the taxpaying public has only limited amounts of generosity, there seems little recourse but to ration funds not only on the basis of total dollar payoffs but also on the ranges in which they occur. For income gains at *some* very high level, an antipoverty justification surely loses its force completely.

Nevertheless, in conducting a war on poverty we cannot ignore other social aims entirely, and they should be integrated in some way with the antipoverty goal. This is true about the nonpecuniary benefits of various programs as well as the pecuniary benefits that happen to occur outside the poverty range. What appear to be the major varieties of "other considerations" are discussed in Chapter 6. Before tackling these additional benefits, we must try to determine the actual efficiency of various types of educational change when they are evaluated from a strictly antipoverty point of view. That is the task of Chapters 3, 4, and 5.

CHAPTER III

Job Training
and Dropout Prevention

In order to compare the efficiency of different types of educational programs in alleviating poverty, it is necessary to find a technique for evaluating the effectiveness of such programs. This chapter develops a methodology for evaluation. The suggested technique is illustrated in this and the two following chapters through specific empirical applications. Policy inferences arising from these illustrations are necessarily heavily qualified because so much of the data used is fragile and imperfect. The reader is urged to focus on the techniques employed, for the specific results are at best suggestive and are certainly not set forth as "final answers."

Five distinctly different types of educational improvement are considered: job retraining for experienced workers and dropout prevention programs, in this chapter; compensatory education programs for "culturally deprived" children and preschool programs, in Chapter 4; increasing the quality and magnitude of resources put into formal education, in Chapter 5. The analysis in this chapter consists of adjusting benefit-cost studies of other authors to make them comparable. In Chapters 4 and 5 the analysis begins with educational data of various sorts, previously unexplored for their benefit-cost implications. For all computations, the general assumptions are uniform; adjustments are made, as best they can be, to allow some comparability even among the most dissimilar types of educational improvements.

The computations are derived from special programs and other educational information that predate the war on poverty. While it would be desirable to use data from the war on poverty itself, at least to supplement the earlier information, the relevant programs have not run long enough to generate usable data on returns. However, there is considerable variety in the programs examined and many of the educational improvements come quite close to the sorts included in current federal efforts.

Comparison of Different Types of Education

One task of these chapters is to rank the various types of education by their apparent degree of efficiency in curing poverty. If the criteria developed in Chapter 2 are accepted, the efficiency ranking would depend not only on the average costs and average returns, but also on the income ranges in which the returns are expected to occur. Nevertheless, for the time being we sidestep the matter of weighting returns according to income range. One reason for this is that in many of the available studies we only have a rough idea whether the variance on income gains is relatively high or relatively low. Moreover, omitting the weighting problem at this stage allows us to isolate and simplify the discussion of other technical and conceptual problems. The question of weighting according to income range is discussed briefly in Chapter 5, where it is asked whether the difference in variance among the different types of education might alter the ranking yielded by unweighted benefit-cost ratios.

A second purpose of this analysis is to estimate whether payoff rates for various types of education are high enough to suggest a heavy education emphasis in the war on poverty. It must be cautioned, however, that the calculations are only a first approach to this issue. Chapter 6 attempts some needed refinements on these calculations and also considers benefits from education other than that of raising the incomes of the poor. These refinements and other benefits also have some bearing on the relative desirability of the various types of education we are about to analyze strictly from an antipoverty perspective.

Our third purpose is to present a methodology that is applicable to the problem at hand. It thus will make clear what types of data should be gathered in the future in order to permit assessment of newer programs on a comparable basis.

Computational Rules

Though a number of important conceptual and empirical problems have not yet been resolved, there is a generally accepted set of ground rules and conventions for benefit-cost estimates of education. Whenever possible, the computations in Chapters 3, 4, and 5 comply with them. Many of the assumptions are peculiar to only one or two types of educational change, and these are discussed as they are encountered. Two that are common to nearly any sort of educational change aimed at reducing poverty are dealt with at the outset. One involves the question of which observable dollar amounts should be counted, and the other is the issue of which discount rate should be used to reduce future dollar amounts to present value. In answering both questions, the general perspective is that of Chapter 2 which considers poverty alleviation as a special variety of "public goods."

In choosing the appropriate dollar costs to take into account, it could be argued that a "representative citizen" should be concerned only with the tax costs of various programs. Thus, if two educational programs yield the same income gain for the poor, it might be thought that the program requiring less public expenditures is the more desirable. This, however, would be an oversight for at least two important, and related, reasons. The poor themselves might have to incur some private expense in order to take advantage of the educational opportunity offered them. Even if society agrees to cover all the direct costs, the poor may have to sacrifice work at gainful employment for the sake of attending classes. Taking only tax costs into account would imply indifference about the indirect expense imposed on the poor.

Related to the question of costs incurred by the poor is the question of what should be done about education programs that include a transfer payment element (for example, a subsistence allowance for a worker who undertakes retraining). Transfers represent an immediate improvement in the well-being of the poor, and this should be of interest to society in the same sense as immediate costs incurred by the poor. The costs of transfer can thus be assumed to be counterbalanced by the immmediate gains. The tax costs of transfers will therefore be excluded in all the following calculations.

On the returns side, similar problems arise. In particular, there is a question of what to do about the taxes paid by the poor as a result of their higher incomes arising from the extra education. From the viewpoint of society, we would surely *not* want to exclude these future taxes since they imply a lighter future tax burden for everyone (for ,a given level of public service). On the other hand, if the income of the poor has risen to taxable levels, there is an implication that the marginal income gains are no longer in the poverty range. The problem is a complex one, depending not only upon the final weighting scheme, but also upon detailed knowledge of the variance of returns. Therefore, in the interests of simplicity, before-tax income gains (unweighted) are used as the measure of returns.[1]

Selecting a discount rate suitable for evaluating antipoverty education is especially hard because two types of present-value calculations are needed. The first involves choosing between education expenditures in the present and transfers (or other direct help) in the future; the second involves comparing returns occurring at different times in the future. In short, we must gauge citizens' preferences for deferring payments and also their degree of impatience for witnessing poverty reduction.

Complete theoretical solutions for the discount problem are still missing;[2] about the only thing that is clear is that the returns from

---

[1] The above procedure is likely to yield somewhat higher benefit-cost ratios than one that diligently followed the framework developed in Chapter 2. On the cost side, the analysis of Chapter 2 would suggest that we weight the private expenses incurred by the poor at something greater than the dollars spent out of public revenues. And since some of the returns will likely occur in relatively high income ranges, the failure to apply weights as suggested in Chapter 2 will lead to a greater benefit figure than if weights were applied.

[2] A sharp clash on discount rates is a regular and predictable feature of conferences on benefit-cost analysis. As yet there is no consensus on which rate to choose and how it should be employed. For example, see Otto Eckstein, "A Survey of the Theory

new government investments should not be discounted by some single, observable market rate of return (for example, the federal bond rate or the return on corporate capital). A much more satisfactory solution is to use some composite of rates that represents the various opportunity costs of foregone investment for different categories of taxpayers. Such a composite would be a fair approximation of the average taxpayer's preference for delaying payments for alleviating poverty. The most careful empirical work on the interest rate lost by a balanced cross-section of taxpayers suggests a discount rate of approximately 5 percent.[3]

For gauging the relative preference for antipoverty returns (resulting from educating the poor) which occur at different points in the future, there is less to go on. Here too, however, a composite relating to various categories of citizens is needed. But pinning down the degree of impatience for witnessing reductions in poverty is no easier than deriving preferences about where lines should be. Hence, in the interest of simplicity, it is assumed that a 5 percent rate applies here as well.

Job Retraining

Of all types of special educational programs applicable to the poor, job retraining has received the most benefit-cost attention. One explanation for this might be that federally sponsored retraining programs were initiated on a reasonably large scale well before the official declaration of the poverty war—under the Area Redevelopment Act (1961) and the Manpower Development and Training Act (1962)[4]—and evaluative data have had some time to

---

of Public Expenditure Criteria," plus comments and rejoinder, in *Public Finances: Needs, Sources, and Utilization* (National Bureau of Economic Research, 1961), p. 439-504; and Burton A. Weisbrod, "Preventing High School Dropouts," plus comments and rejoinder, in Robert Dorfman (ed.), *Measuring Benefits of Government Investments* (Brookings Institution, 1965), pp. 117-71.

[3] John V. Krutilla and Otto Eckstein, *Multiple Purpose River Development* (Johns Hopkins Press, 1957), Chap. 4.

[4] See U.S. Department of Labor, *Manpower Report of the President and Report on Manpower Requirements, Resources, Utilization and Training, 1966*.

accumulate. Perhaps a more important reason is the apparent research advantages in an educational process that runs a relatively short time and whose participants enter (or return to) the job market more or less immediately. Both the costs of the program and some indication of actual returns are events occurring in a contemporary economic context, thereby offering the hope of keeping risky assumptions to a minimum. Nevertheless, to bridge the gap between raw data and policy choice, a number of assumptions are still needed; and the empirical (and/or theoretical) grounds for making these assumptions are often not very firm.

This difficulty is amply reflected in the three most detailed case studies of job retraining programs. The studies concentrate on retraining experience in three states—Connecticut, West Virginia, and Massachusetts—each study focusing on one state.[5] In all three the central purpose is to estimate social efficiency by comparing training costs with the resulting time-discounted gain in before-tax earnings. In deriving earnings estimates they rely on surveys of workers conducted approximately one year after retraining and attempt to extrapolate these short-run observations well into the fu-

[5] David A. Page, "Retraining Under the Manpower Development Act: A Cost-Benefit Analysis," *Public Policy*, Vol. 13 (1964), pp. 257-67 (Brookings Reprint No. 86), cited hereinafter as Page, Massachusetts study; Gerald G. Somers and Ernst W. Stromsdorfer, "A Benefit-Cost Analysis of Manpower Retraining," in Gerald G. Somers (ed.), *Proceedings of the Seventeenth Annual Meeting*, Industrial Relations Research Association (Madison, Wisconsin, 1965), pp. 172-85, cited hereinafter as Somers and Stromsdorfer, West Virginia study; and Michael E. Borus, "A Benefit-Cost Analysis of the Economic Effectiveness of Retraining the Unemployed," *Yale Economic Essays*, Vol. 4, No. 2 (Fall 1964), pp. 371-430, cited hereinafter as Borus, Connecticut study. Each of the programs was planned and initiated by the respective state. In Massachusetts the program was entirely state operated and financed; the other two states collaborated with the Area Redevelopment Administration. The study covered 438 trainees in Connecticut, 259 in West Virginia, and 152 in Massachusetts. Diversity in the mix of course offerings in the three programs presumably was due to the peculiarities of local job markets as perceived by state employment authorities. Most of the workers interviewed in Connecticut were trained in machine shop operations, pipefitting, and shipfitting. Over half of the Massachusetts group was enrolled in schools for barbers and technicians, and the rest were spread over a wide variety of fields from drafting to auto repair (Page, Massachusetts study, p. 266). The West Virginia program "included auto repair, construction trades, electrical maintenance, machine tool operators, riveters, welders; and for women, nurses aides, typists-stenographers, and waitresses" (Somers and Stromsdorfer, West Virginia study, p. 173).

TABLE 2

Estimates of Benefits and Costs of Retraining, per Worker, in
Independent Studies in Three States[a]

Study	Benefits	Costs	Benefit-Cost Ratio
Connecticut[b]	$29,965	$218	137.3
Massachusetts[c]	4,299	698	6.1
West Virginia[d]	8,990	693	12.9

[a] Sources: Page, Massachusetts study; Somers and Stromsdorfer, West Virginia study; and Borus, Connecticut study (see note 5, p. 39, for full reference). All three studies experiment to some extent with alternative assumptions. The range of estimates within each study is very small, however, in relation to the range among the studies, and the values in the table are fairly representative of alternative values within the studies.

[b] See Connecticut study, pp. 403, 413, 418.

[c] The Massachusetts study originally performed the computations in terms of aggregate benefits and costs for all workers taken together. The conversion to per-worker benefits is consistent with the per-worker estimates found in the other studies. See p. 263 for original benefit estimates and pp. 260-61 for original cost estimates.

[d] Benefits and costs are weighted averages of results for males and females. Benefit figures are from the West Virginia study, pp. 182-83; cost figures are derived from data on p. 181.

ture. As illustrated in Table 2, all three arrive at the same general answer: the gain in earnings clearly exceeds the cost of retraining. But marring this happy concurrence is the very large disparity in the size of the computed ratios—the highest ratio being over twenty times greater than the lowest. Interestingly enough, very little of the disparity is traceable to the raw data. Indeed, nearly all of it, as we shall see, is a result of the different assumptions used in converting the raw numbers into estimates of benefits and costs.

While even the most pessimistic study arrives at a ratio that indicates that retraining is considerably more effective than transfers, it would seem worthwhile to attempt a resolution, or at least a compromise settlement, of the assumptions that create the divergent results. Narrowing the range of plausible estimates would let us know how great is the "margin of safety" and would also come in handy in the course of ranking educational improvements according to their economic efficiency.

Part of the conflict on assumptions involves the computational rules adopted in the introduction of this chapter and hence can be resolved summarily. The greatest departure from these rules occurs in the Massachusetts study where transfer payments in the form of subsistence allowances were counted along with the actual resource costs of training and where a 10 percent discount rate was used to relate returns to costs.[6] Dropping the subsistence costs and substituting a 5 percent rate both act to raise the benefit-cost ratio, the combined effect bringing this ratio very close to the ratio in the West Virginia study. Deviations in the West Virginia study are minor: a small amount of subsistence costs is included and a 4 percent discount rate is employed. Corrections for these practically cancel one another.[7]

Although the Connecticut study conforms to our general computational rules, it contains one clearly inappropriate computational twist: the application of a national income multiplier to the estimated gain in earnings flowing directly from retraining. While this might be a legitimate procedure if the choice were between retraining and doing nothing at all, it is not appropriate if we assume that transfer payments or other types of education will be undertaken if retraining is not. Any type of new expenditure can generate a multiplier effect. To say that retraining is an especially desirable sort of expenditure, it must be shown that it can stand on its own feet, that is, that the direct gains are sufficient to more than cover the costs.[8]

Eliminating the multiplier from the Connecticut figure reduces the benefit-cost ratio to nearly half its original value. But the resulting ratio still remains well above the ratios in the other two studies. The major cause for the remaining difference is easy to locate. Its resolution is difficult.

[6] Page, Massachusetts study, pp. 260, 264.

[7] Somers and Stromsdorfer, West Virginia study, pp. 180, 182. These corrections, and those for the Massachusetts study, are included in the revised estimates presented in Table 3.

[8] It should be noted also that the income generated through the multiplier has no clear, measurable effect on poverty. Some of it may result in new and better jobs for the poor, but a large portion may not. Finally, it must be remembered that the generation of new aggregate demand through the multiplier can be considered a favorable development only if it is thought desirable to push the economy toward higher levels of activity. If, at a given point in time, the economy is thought to be already "overheated," the demand induced by the multiplier is something we would rather be without.

It is clear enough that, even after eliminating the multiplier, the main source of the divergence is imbedded somewhere in the returns side of the analysis. In computing returns, all three studies begin with the yearly earnings of the retrained employees as reported on questionnaire surveys. The West Virginia and Massachusetts studies, at this point, introduce earnings data derived from surveys of workers who were not retrained but who had past employment histories and other characteristics similar to those of workers who were retrained.[9] These workers are used as control groups to estimate how the typical trainee would have fared in the same period had he remained untrained. The average earnings of the control group are subtracted from the average earnings of the retrained workers, and the difference is recorded as the net gain resulting from retraining.[10] The Connecticut study, on the other hand, makes no such subtraction, even though it contains the information to do so. The reason given is that excess demand persists in the occupations for which workers were retrained, but excess supplies of workers are apparently available for most unskilled and semiskilled occupations.[11] If this is true, then retraining a worker does not mean that the job he would have held otherwise —if he was lucky enough to be employed—remains vacant. Rather, the vacant post is easily and quickly filled by someone who is unemployed and would have remained unemployed had the opening not occurred. Thus, it is argued, the net gain in total income for all workers is equal to the entire earnings for the persons retrained and successfully placed.

In brief, the Connecticut study assumes that each successfully trained person reduces by one the total of unemployed persons. This assumption might therefore be categorized by saying that existing unemployment is essentially "structural" in nature. But then, how might we label the assumptions about unemployment found in the other two studies?

---

[9] Somers and Stromsdorfer, West Virginia study, pp. 173, 182; Page, Massachusetts study, pp. 262-64.

[10] The Massachusetts study accomplishes this in a slightly more roundabout way (see pp. 262-63).

[11] Borus, Connecticut study, p. 399. The earnings of nontrainees are used in another part of the study where the aim is to estimate the net *private* gain to the trainee.

Here, too, it is assumed that total unemployment is reduced as a result of retraining. The reduction in these two studies is measured by the difference in unemployment rates between retrainees and control groups. This is implicit in the simple subtraction of control group earnings from the earnings of trainees since it was not full-time earnings that were used for the subtraction, but rather, total earnings over a given period of time. This means of gauging unemployment reduction is much less optimistic than the Connecticut method. Instead of assuming that each retrained worker results in one more person employed, it assumes only that the average trainee is employed for a little longer portion of the year without affecting the employment available to other workers. There is no presumption that excess supply can be identified for some occupations and excess demand for others. Rather, it is implicitly asserted that retraining improves the labor market only in the sense that the retrained workers find jobs a little more easily and quickly, and spend less time in transition between jobs. Thus, in the absence of a better way to pigeonhole this assumption, we might say that different rates of "frictional" unemployment apply to the two different groups of workers.[12]

Having located the major source of disagreement as an unemployment question, it must now be asked how it can be resolved. Not much help can be expected from the general literature on the nature of recent unemployment. The empirical work here is too crude in its occupational breakdowns, and there is no way to determine whether a clever prognosis of job openings for certain narrow types of skills—matched with the appropriate types of retraining—makes a one-to-one improvement in employment figures or,

[12] It is interesting to note at this point that the Massachusetts study (p. 266) and the West Virginia study (p. 174) also worried about the indirect repercussions on the employment situation of workers other than those immediately observed. But their concern was with a possible *overestimate* of the employment effect. It was speculated that some of the retrained workers may have displaced workers who could have performed the same jobs with equal competence, thereby giving an upward bias to the simple subtraction of control group earnings from trainee earnings. In other words, there was a suspicion that excess supplies of workers existed for all occupations—that is, that existing unemployment was essentially aggregate demand unemployment. The hypothesis is never totally rejected, though the studies rest content with the simple subtraction on the grounds that insufficient information exists to verify the displacement hypothesis.

instead, improves the job market and the employment rate in a more modest way. The three case studies also provide only limited information to arbitrate this matter. They were done roughly simultaneously and each without cognizance, apparently, of the assumptions used in the others. A debate was not joined over the disagreement just noted. Still, scattered pieces of information in these studies can be brought to bear as circumstantial evidence on the unemployment question. Most of the useful information is in the Connecticut study, and it casts doubt on the legitimacy of making no deduction at all from the total earnings of the retrained.

First of all, a number of observed phenomena serve to weaken the argument that anyone could perform at the job that a retrained worker foregoes in accepting employment in a training-related occupation. For instance, both the Connecticut and Massachusetts studies note that among the workers who completed retraining a good number went back to previously held jobs which were unrelated to the training received.[13] Presumably their experience at these jobs made these workers more adept and more valuable than entirely new employees. It seems fair to assume that still more of these workers would have returned to old jobs if they had not had retraining. If these inferences are correct, it would not then be safe to assume that all openings created by retraining were promptly filled by workers of identical productivity. A related piece of evidence is the interesting finding in the Connecticut study that the hourly wage for the control group of nontrainees was about the same as the hourly wage of those retrained.[14] If wage rate is thought to be reflective of the amount of human investment required to do a job, it would follow that the jobs held by nontrainees required as much background skill as did the retrained-for occupations.[15] This, too, seems to indicate that not every employed worker could fill the vacancies resulting from retraining.

[13] Borus, Connecticut study, pp. 376, 390; Page, Massachusetts study, p. 262.

[14] Borus, Connecticut study, p. 381.

[15] The Connecticut study found that two groups of workers who did not complete retraining courses had higher total earnings during the time period than workers who were retrained. These two groups consisted of workers who qualified for, but did not enter the course because they found employment for which retraining was not necessary and those who entered but did not complete the course because they found jobs unrelated to the training. (*Ibid.*, p. 374.)

Another assumption critical to the computational procedure of the Connecticut study is that abundant openings existed in the occupations related to the retraining and that these would have continued to exist if it were not for retraining. But this assumption is called into question by information, in both the Massachusetts and Connecticut studies, indicating that approximately 20 percent of the workers who completed retraining did not secure employment utilizing skills taught in the retraining courses.[16] Though the Connecticut study does not provide a breakdown of the reasons for this, the Massachusetts study does. It reported that "the primary reason (33 percent) given by trainees for not finding a job related to their training was the absence of vacancies, as evidenced by unsuccessful applications to different firms," thus indicating that excess demands may not have been the rule for all trained-for occupations.[17] Equally interesting is the discovery, in the Connecticut study, that 19 percent of the workers in the control group managed to find employment in occupations for which retrainees were being prepared.[18] It might, therefore, be speculated that each retrainee did not fill a position that would otherwise have remained vacant. There is, thus, the implication that some of the trainees acquired their new positions at the expense of workers who were not retrained.

From these and other bits of information in the case studies one cannot perceive a clear and contradiction-free picture. Nevertheless, it is difficult to be sanguine about making no subtraction at all from the total earnings of those who were trained and placed in training-related occupations. There are, therefore, grounds for reducing still further the estimate of returns found in the Connecticut study. Moreover, if it is thought that excess supply of labor was not the uniform rule for all jobs that untrained workers could perform, it follows that at least some part of the earnings sacrificed by the retrainees while learning new skills should be counted as costs; the income experience of control groups indicates that the lost income was not insubstantial. Costs for the Connecticut program, as they appear in Table 2, make no allowance for this.

[16] Borus, Connecticut study, p. 390; Page, Massachusetts study, p. 262.
[17] Page, Massachusetts study, p. 262.
[18] Borus, Connecticut study, p. 389.

With the available data it is not possible to go much further in setting an upper bound to the payoff rate for job retraining. While there are indications that some deduction should be made from the earnings of retrained workers, it is not possible to say precisely how much (nor, similarly, how much of the apparent income foregone should be added in as costs). Neither is it clear whether the same subtraction procedure should be used for all three retraining programs. Differences in the local job markets and in the training programs may warrant different assumptions. There is, however, no sure way to establish this from the information presented in the studies.

Despite the fact that only limited progress has been made in lowering the upper bound, one might at least take comfort in the conclusion that payoffs to retraining *may* be as high as fifty times costs.[19] This implies it is a greatly more efficient means than direct redistribution for helping low-paid and unemployed workers. A closer look at the lower bound reveals, however, that things are not all that secure. A combination of the most pessimistic assumptions in the three studies can push benefit-cost ratios to levels considerably lower than any mentioned so far.

First, it should be noted that the Massachusetts study (as well as

---

[19] Indeed, the payoff rate may be higher still—even without the influence of the national income multiplier. The Connecticut study did not use the most optimistic set of plausible assumptions. In particular, it projected no growth in earnings in future time periods and assumed a time horizon of only ten years, after which zero benefits were expected to accrue (Borus, Connecticut study, pp. 401-02). Given the rest of the Connecticut assumptions, it is puzzling that earnings were not assumed to expand over the coming years. One might reasonably argue that income *differentials* between trainees and nontrainees may stay the same or shrink, but if one feels that returns are measured by the entire earned income of the successfully placed trainees, it would seem a safe prediction that this will grow. Attrition rates out of the trained-for occupations must, of course, be taken into account, and the Connecticut study does so—and, indeed, even projects them into the future (*ibid.*, p. 403). The failure to project income growth seems quite inconsistent. The ten-year time horizon can only be described as arbitrary. In its defense, the study states only that "it is unlikely that any workers who enter retraining calculate the resulting benefits for more than ten years" (*ibid.*, p. 388). This statement occurs in a section devoted to estimating private returns; the transference of the assumption to the social returns section is undefended. It is interesting that both the West Virginia study (pp. 181-82) and the Massachusetts study (p. 264) employ a time horizon encompassing the remaining working life of the trainee.

the Connecticut study[20]) makes no allowance for the earnings foregone by trainees while attending classes. Since it subtracted control group earnings from the earnings of trainees, the failure to make an estimate of this cost appears to be a clear inconsistency. Thus, it seems more reasonable to include an estimate of this cost as did the West Virginia study.

Second, it should not be supposed that the estimate in the West Virginia study was uniformly more pessimistic in its assumptions than were the other studies. Indeed, on at least one important assumption, it was considerably more charitable. In counting the gains from retraining, it was the only study that presumed that placement in a training-related occupation was *not* a necessary condition for demonstrating that retraining did indeed benefit a given worker. In other words, no distinction was made between those who were placed in training-related occupations and those who were not. Since other evidence indicates that trainees not placed in training-related jobs still earned more than control groups with no retraining,[21] inclusion of their earnings in the calculation implies a higher average returns estimate than when they are excluded, as they are in the other two studies.

Third, there is the question of how far into the future one should extrapolate returns. The West Virginia and Massachusetts studies assume that the short-run income gains persist throughout the workers' entire lifetime, and indeed may grow.[22] The Connecticut study, on the other hand, points out that some attrition can be expected as some of the trained-for jobs obsolesce and as workers depart voluntarily for other occupations. It also assumes a time horizon of only ten years.[23] Applying these two assumptions to the Massachusetts and West Virginia studies would reduce appreciably their estimated returns.

If one combines the most pessimistic assumptions in the three studies, the resulting benefit-cost ratios could be reduced to a level not much above unity. And, at least for the Massachusetts pro-

---

[20] See Borus, Connecticut study, pp. 378-83.

[21] Page, Massachusetts study, p. 260.

[22] Somers and Stromsdorfer, West Virginia study, pp. 181-83; Page, Massachusetts study, pp. 264-65.

[23] Borus, Connecticut study, pp. 393, 399. See note 19, p. 46.

gram, it can be demonstrated that the ratio could be pushed below unity if one employs the harshest (but still plausible) assumptions about the magnitude of earnings foregone.

But combining these assumptions would appear no more defensible than using the "no subtraction" procedure of the Connecticut study. In the first place, excluding trainees who were not placed in training-related occupations would not seem entirely consistent. If it is thought reasonable to subtract control group earnings from the earnings of "successfully placed" trainees, this implies a trust in the "representativeness" of the control group, that it represents fairly what trainees would have earned if left untrained. It will be remembered, however, that trainees not placed in trained-for occupations end up earning more than control groups. If this apparent gain is not real, there is then not much reason to have confidence in the apparent gains recorded by the "successfully placed" trainees.[24]

The use of a ten-year time horizon is also a dubious assumption. The Connecticut study does not give a convincing defense for this, and it would seem much more reasonable to apply a lifetime horizon as was done in the other two studies.[25]

Thus, if we are to base our benefit-cost figures on some sort of differential income estimate—and the analysis of the Connecticut study suggests that we should—the simple subtraction of control group earnings from the earnings of all trainees, combined with a lifetime horizon, appears to be the least arbitrary procedure. Table 3 presents the results of applying that procedure, as consistently as possible, to all three studies. The estimates here assume

[24] The Connecticut study (p. 376) argues that individuals who completed training were probably more intelligent and ambitious than nontrainees, even though the two groups were matched according to education, employment history, and several other individual characteristics. It is argued that this, plus the likelihood that the state employment agencies exercised favoritism toward trainees, explains the apparent income gain by those working in non-training related fields. The West Virginia study, on the other hand, contends that all trainees picked up some versatility and improved work habits that were valuable even in tasks not specifically related to their training (Somers and Stormsdorfer, West Virginia study, p. 175). The truth is undoubtedly somewhere between these two positions. But the available information offers no way to settle on a nonarbitrary compromise.

[25] See note 19, p. 46.

TABLE 3

Adjusted Estimates of Benefits and Costs of Retraining, per Worker, Presented in Table 2

Study	Benefits[a]	Costs[b]	Benefit-Cost Ratio
Connecticut	$6,852	$ 680	10.1
Massachusetts	9,805	2,361	4.2
West Virginia	9,034	602	15.0

[a] All calculations are based on the mean earnings differentials between all trainees and their corresponding control groups, as originally reported in the three studies. (See Page, Massachusetts study, pp. 262-65; Somers and Stromsdorfer, West Virginia study, p. 180; and Borus, Connecticut study, pp. 379-82.) For the West Virginia study, the weighted average benefit of male and female trainees was used. For the Connecticut study, weighted averages also had to be calculated to merge the trainees "utilizing" and those "not utilizing" their training. Control groups here were originally divided into those "who refused retraining for employment" and those who refused without an employment prospect. A weighted average was used here as well. Differentials appearing in the original studies were assumed to remain constant until retirement at the (assumed) age of 65. The average age at time of retraining was assumed to be 30. This was the approximate average age of trainees in the Connecticut (p. 390) and Massachusetts (p. 264) programs. (The West Virginia study did not provide information on this.) Benefit streams were adjusted for mortality (based on U.S. Department of Commerce, Bureau of the Census, *Statistical Abstract of the United States, 1965*, Table 60, p. 54). They were then discounted by a 5 percent rate.

[b] Summation of direct cost and earnings foregone. The direct cost component of this figure comes from estimates originally presented in the three studies. (Borus, Connecticut study, p. 418; Page, Massachusetts study, pp. 260-61; Somers and Stromsdorfer, West Virginia study, pp. 180-81.) All transfer payments to trainees are excluded. Earnings foregone are based on the earnings of control groups during the time period when trainees were in training. (Borus, Connecticut study, pp. 379-82; Page, Massachusetts study, pp. 262-63; Somers and Stromsdorfer, West Virginia study, p. 181.) For Connecticut and West Virginia weighted averages of earnings rates (see note a) were combined with information on length of time of the training program. The Massachusetts study did not report the duration of the training program; it was therefore assumed that duration was directly proportional to direct costs. Since the Massachusetts program was about five times more expensive in direct cost terms than the Connecticut program, it was estimated that it also lasted five times longer. The resulting figure was 31 weeks. This was then multiplied by an estimate of weekly rates of foregone earnings.

no growth or shrinkage in earnings differentials (that is, yearly benefits) over time: a tendency for some trainees to improve upon their short-run gains is assumed to be exactly counterbalanced by a tendency for others to lose at least part of their initial earnings advantage as their occupations undergo "obsolescence" in future periods. An estimate for earnings foregone during retraining is also included in these calculations. All benefit streams are adjusted for mortality and discounted by 5 percent.

The adjusted benefit-cost ratios in Table 3 are all well in excess of unity. Like the original estimates, they indicate that retraining is a socially profitable undertaking. The table also illustrates that the differences among estimates in the original studies were largely a matter of differing assumptions.[26] There is of course no guarantee that precisely the same assumptions are appropriate for every retraining program (although there is no convincing evidence to the contrary), nor is it clear that the assumptions behind Table 3 are the very best possible. Yet, they appear more defensible than the other ready alternatives, and as we shall see, are the ones most consistent with the assumptions adopted in Chapters 4 and 5.

Though the benefit-cost history of job retraining, as conducted prior to the war on poverty, indicates that this sort of program "pays for itself," it must still be asked whether this conclusion holds in the present antipoverty context. Among the chief worries here is whether favorable benefit-cost ratios will hold for youths newly entering the labor market and for the "hard core" unemployed. Another is whether new programs like Neighborhood Youth Corps and Job Corps, having characteristics somewhat different from the Manpower Development and Training programs, will show up as well as the earlier programs. On the former question, there is some evidence indicating youths respond more favorably than the typical trainee and that the hard core unemployed (older workers, workers who have experienced exceedingly long periods of unemployment, and workers with very low educational attainments) respond less favorably.[27] Firm conclusions on these subgroups are, however, not yet possible. And, evaluation of the economic effectiveness of the new types of programs must await the generation of evaluative data from those programs.[28]

[26] Several things could account for the remaining differences in the ratios. Sampling variability, differences in the adequacy of the control groups, different cost accounting procedures, and actual differences in efficiency are all likely involved.

[27] Borus, Connecticut study, pp. 390-418. The breakdowns in the Connecticut study, as they relate to youths, did not go beyond specifying a group twenty years of age or younger. It was not stated how many of these, if any, had no previous work experience. Other data indicate that approximately 10 percent of the enrollees in Manpower Development programs, nationwide, were new entrants into the labor market. See U.S. Department of Labor, *Manpower Research and Training Under the Manpower Development and Training Act* (1964), pp. 38-39.

[28] It might also be wondered what the implications are of labor markets that are

Dropout Prevention

Great importance has been assigned by many writers and educators to the goal of reducing the high school dropout rate. In 1962, with the initiation of a special Presidential fund to support dropout prevention programs, it became a matter of official federal concern. The widely expressed interest in the problem has been mirrored in the large number of anti-dropout programs that sprang up across the country in the early 1960's.[29] And the interest has followed through into the war on poverty: both the Neighborhood Youth Corps and the Job Corps concentrate heavily on high school dropouts.

As noted in the first chapter, school continuance per se has not held center stage in the education programs connected with the war on poverty. Still, dropout prevention is a component of some of these programs, and it would be desirable if the efficiency of this component could be estimated. In gauging efficiency, one could simply rely on the sort of evidence discussed in Chapter 1. This, however, presumes that reducing dropout rates entails no extra costs, that it involves either costless encouragement or simple improvements in the flexibility of capital markets.[30] It is not at all

tighter than those of 1961-63, the period when the retraining studies were performed. On the one hand, it could be argued that training and retraining workers is complementary with a higher level of economic activity and tighter labor markets. Under these conditions, trainees are more likely to find jobs in the trained-for occupations, and this in turn may help to break some troublesome labor bottlenecks. On the other hand, it might be noted that a large part of the estimated return from retraining can be traced to different rates of unemployment between skilled and unskilled workers and that this difference typically narrows when the economy is at higher levels of activity. The estimate of returns might therefore indicate that retraining is less efficient during periods of high overall employment. Thus, it might be argued that retraining and tight labor markets are, to some extent, substitute policies.

[29] For some idea of the scope and variety of these programs, see U.S. Department of Health, Education, and Welfare, Office of Education, *Selected Reports and Statistics on High School Dropouts*, OE-20063 (1964).

[30] As noted earlier, the only serious financial constraint possibly deterring the completion of public schooling is the income foregone by the postponement of entry into the labor market. The problem of making loans for this sort of expense seems no more difficult than for direct costs of schooling. The youthfulness of the "in-

clear that the current efforts to prevent dropouts can be considered costless. Indeed, they appear to be founded on the supposition that the potential dropout requires intensive counseling and persuasion to be induced to stay until high school graduation and to learn as much during this period as a typical high school graduate.[31]

To find out the typical cost, and payoff, of dropout prevention programs, there is even less to go on than in the case of job retraining. As late as August 1967 the only published case study of benefits and costs was on a program conducted in St. Louis in 1960-62.[32] It is not at all clear that this program was a representative one. Work orientation was not nearly so important as it is in the Neighborhood Youth Corps or the Job Corps. The intensity

---

vestor" does, however, lead to complications. For college education, the most interesting proposals for surmounting the risk problems of financing human capital involve government loans repaid through future income taxes. Such schemes gear the amount of loan repayment to the magnitude of the future income of the person educated. It is not apparent, however, how this (or similar schemes) can be adapted to the legal minor and how responsibilities are to be shared between parent and pupil. For a description of self-financing government loans on the college level, see William Vickery, "A Proposal for Student Loans," in Selma J. Mushkin (ed.), *Economics of Higher Education* (U.S. Department of Health, Education, and Welfare, Office of Education, 1962), pp. 268-80; and Milton Friedman, "The Role of Government in Education," in *Capitalism and Freedom* (University of Chicago Press, 1962), pp. 98-107.

[31] The emphasis on correcting "detrimental" attitudes receives some justification from studies on factors causing students to leave high school. Though none of these studies focuses exclusively on poverty stricken students, it is interesting to note that students and high school counselors do not often assign much importance to purely economic elements. The most important reason seems to be the students' open dislike for school. Counselors also cite unfavorable parental attitudes toward education. (See Michigan Employment Security Commission, Detroit Board of Education, *The Detroit High School Leaver Project: Final Report* [October 1964], pp. 86-88; Lorne H. Woollatt, "Why Capable Students Drop Out of High School," *Bulletin of the National Association of Secondary Principals*, Vol. 45, No. 268 [November 1961], pp. 1-8; and *Manpower Report of the President, 1966*, p. 93.) This does not mean that straightforward financial inducements could not reduce the dropout rate significantly. It does suggest, though, that if no change in attitude takes place, the would-be dropouts will not likely acquire a gain in learning comparable to that of the typical high school graduate. This implies, in turn, that the later-life income differential between dropouts and graduates could not very well be used as a measure of returns, even if one did control for "ability" and socioeconomic background.

[32] The study involved an "experimental" group of 429 students and a "control" group of 385. By the end of two years, 189 or 44.1 percent in the experimental group

and costs of this program cannot even be established as typical of a more conventional dropout prevention program. Nevertheless, the study merits consideration if for no other reason than that costs were found to exceed benefits, thereby shedding doubt on the relevance of the many previous calculations that indicated that payoff rates for not dropping out of high school are safely high. It is estimated, by Weisbrod, that each rescued dropout earns an average of $3,427 more as a result of going through until graduation, but that the reduction in the dropout rate, as a result of the program, was so low that each rescue cost $8,200.[33]

The case study is generally orthodox in its procedures and complies with the computational rules established at the beginning of this chapter. Actual resource costs, estimated lifetime income gain of the saved dropouts, and a 5 percent discount rate are the essential elements. The dropout program examined seems respectable enough: it received the blessing and financial support of the Ford Foundation and, from its description, appears to have been well organized and carefully tended. Over 400 potential dropouts were treated with the special program (a larger sample than any of the retraining studies) and they were matched with a control group with similar attributes who received only ordinary services. In all, it seems as careful an experiment and case study as could be expected on a short-term basis.

There are, however, some computational issues on the returns side of the analysis that merit discussion, not only because of their importance to the study itself, but also because of similar problems found in Chapters 4 and 5.

First, it should be noted that, unlike the retraining studies, the dropout study did not actually observe individuals affected by the program when they appeared in the labor force. Rather, the dropouts who were saved were simply assumed to be as economically

---

had dropped out, as compared with 200 or 52.0 percent of the control group. This 7.9 percent difference, representing 34 students, was assumed to be the number of dropouts prevented by the program. (Burton A. Weisbrod, "Preventing High School Dropouts," in Robert Dorfman [ed.], *Measuring Benefits of Government Investments* [Brookings Institution, 1965], pp. 117-49.)

[33] Amounts here are in terms of 1960 dollars. The corresponding figures based on 1949 prices (the base year used by Weisbrod) are $2,750 and $6,540, respectively (*ibid.*, p. 148).

successful throughout their lives as typical high school graduates currently in the labor force, as calculated from income data in the U.S. census. Similarly, it was assumed that dropping out of high school would have meant a lifetime income equal to that of a typical dropout now in the labor force (also calculated from census data). Though the failure to actually witness the income experience of the people directly affected is an unfortunate shortcoming, the use of census data does entail some distinct advantages. Most importantly, census data provide a basis for estimating the entire lifetime income stream of dropouts and graduates. Unlike the retraining studies, one need not rely on the income differences that emerge shortly after the termination of education as a gauge of what will occur later in life.

The comparison of census income streams does, however, present difficulties with employment assumptions that are similar to those observed in the retraining section. Unemployment rates are substantially higher among high school dropouts than among graduates, and once more one is faced with postulating the nature of unemployment. Weisbrod simply subtracts the census income stream of an average dropout from that of the graduate and thereby assumes (in essence) that the lower unemployment rate of graduates will apply to the saved dropout without any negative or positive employment effects on other members of the labor force. This assumption is no more easily defended than it was in the retraining studies. Its chief virtue is that it has greater plausibility than the other two ready assumptions: that a saved dropout means full employment for one person who would have been "fully" unemployed, or that absolutely no improvement in employment occurs.[34] While there is no guarantee that the improvement in labor markets is accurately measured by the differential unemploy-

---

[34] An assumption that no net improvement occurs in unemployment as a result of extra education would make it difficult to demonstrate that any dropout prevention program could be profitable. As in the case of retrained and unretrained workers, there is evidence that hourly wage rates are not much different between dropouts and graduates. Of particular interest on this point is the sample survey by Morgan and David. They found the average hourly wage differential to be so small that if both dropouts and graduates were employed full time and if one takes into account the two years extra worked by dropouts, the *un*discounted lifetime income streams of the two groups are practically the same. Thus, any direct costs for education or for a dropout prevention program would immediately imply a benefit-cost

ment rates between graduates and dropouts, it would nevertheless appear to be the only "compromise" assumption that does not require arbitrary adjustments.

If we settle on the simple procedure of subtracting income streams, there is still the question of which income streams to use. Weisbrod's study relied on the 1950 census (the most recent then available), whose only suitable figures related to (non-South) median total income. The 1960 census now provides a whole menu of possible differentials that could legitimately be applied to dropout programs in St. Louis. Among the leading options are: (1) median total income in the northcentral section of the United States; (2) median total income in central cities; (3) median earned income in the non-South; (4) mean earned income in the non-South. Since the dropout prevention program under consideration occurred in the 1960-62 period, it seems preferable to use the more recent census information. Moreover, the availability of earnings data and of more specific demographic breakdowns in the 1960 census provide added reason for using the later numbers.

Table 4 shows the results of computing the present values for two of the 1960 census streams and how these answers compare with the computations based on the 1950 census. These values relate, respectively, to 1959 and 1949 earnings (and income). The two 1959 values turn out to be quite similar; and though the resulting benefit-cost ratios are higher than that for 1949, they still fail to exceed unity.[35] The values based on 1959 earnings seem to

---

ratio less than one. (James Morgan and Martin David, "Education and Income," *Quarterly Journal of Economics,* Vol. 77, No. 3 [August 1963], p. 434.)

The other possible assumption—that a saved dropout means that net employment is increased by one full worker—is even more dubious here than in the case of job retraining. While one might argue that some highly specialized occupations, related specifically to job retraining, are characterized by an abundant excess demand for workers, it is difficult to make a similar claim about ordinary high school graduates. This does not imply that the actual improvement in net employment cannot be something greater than that indicated by the differential unemployment rates between graduates and dropouts. But, keeping in mind the alternative possibility that graduates might simply displace equally capable dropouts (as discussed in Chap. 1), the simple subtraction procedure appears to be much closer to the truth. On this score, it might be mentioned that the payoff rate studies on school continuation, cited in Chap. 1, all employed a simple subtraction procedure.

[35] The same types of computations for the other two possible 1960 bases would yield lower ratios than those in Table 4. This is indicated by the yearly income and

TABLE 4

Benefit-Cost Estimates of St. Louis Dropout Prevention Program, Based on Selected Income Streams[a]

Income Stream	Financial Value of Not Dropping Out of High School[b]	Benefit-Cost Ratio at Cost of $8,200 per Prevented Dropout
1949 median income, North and West[c]	$3,427	0.42
1959 median income, central cities[d]	5,261	0.64
1959 mean earnings, North and West[e]	5,673	0.69

[a] Based on estimates of Weisbrod, in "Preventing High School Dropouts." All values are expressed in terms of 1960 dollars.

[b] Lifetime differences between high school dropouts and graduates, adjusted for mortality rates with retirement assumed to take place at age 65, and discounted by 5 percent. The individuals treated included more males than females and slightly more nonwhite than white students. Weisbrod computed the increase in the discounted income streams for each possible type of rescued dropout (white-male, white-female, nonwhite-male, nonwhite-female) and then derived a weighted average according to the percentage of each type who were successfully prevented from dropping out. All values in this column are net of the income lost while attending two years of high school.

[c] As computed in *ibid.*, p. 148, adjusted by the increase in the consumer price index from 1949 to 1959.

[d] Computed from *U.S. Census of Population: 1960*, PC(2)-5B, Tables 6 and 7.

[e] Based on Herman P. Miller, in "Lifetime Income and Economic Growth," and supplemented by his *Income Distribution in the United States* (U.S. Department of Commerce, 1966). The type of worker sampled and the definition of yearly earnings are the same as appear in *U.S. Census of Population: 1960*, PC(2)-7B. For workers between 16 and 18 years of age, no comparable figures were available on a mean earnings basis; hence, median income figures were used for "North Central United States" as appear in *ibid.*, PC(2)-5B, Table 6. These come out to a weighted average of $580. Earnings of females were also unavailable; the relationship of female earnings differentials to male earnings differentials (dropouts compared to graduates) was assumed to be the same as the relationship between female *income* differentials to male *income* differentials. In both the 1950 and 1960 censuses, the discounted differentials for females (white and nonwhite) proved to be about 40 percent higher than the discounted differentials for males. Thus, to compute the weighted earnings value for 1960, the discounted earnings gains for white and nonwhite males were multiplied by 1.4 to derive values for their female counterparts.

earnings differences, between dropouts and graduates, for all males over 25, as follows: north and west U.S. (mean earnings), $637; central cities (median income), $538; northcentral U.S. (median income), $432; north and west U.S. (median earnings), $402 (U.S. Department of Commerce, Bureau of the Census, *U.S. Census of Population: 1960*, "Educational Attainment," PC[2]-5B, Table 6; and Herman P. Miller, "Lifetime Income and Economic Growth," *American Economic Review*, Vol. 55, No. 4 [September 1965], pp. 834-44).

represent the fairest comparison with the values computed for retraining. (The retraining data were also in the form of mean earnings, and the observation of the results of retraining programs occurred shortly after 1960.) Though the benefit-cost ratio derived from 1960 earnings data is the highest of those computed, it still falls considerably short of the ratios for retraining estimated in a comparable manner.

It might now be asked, however, whether further sophistication can make a substantial difference in the estimate of returns for not dropping out of high school. The recent work by Gary Becker and others[36] permits some adjustment of returns which might raise benefits above (or at least much closer to) costs.

The two possible adjustments that seem most important involve (1) the predicted future growth in income differentials and (2) the differences in ability and social background between typical graduates and dropouts. Thought the studies relating to these two factors have been far from definitive, they do allow a rough approximation of how much the benefit-cost estimates would be changed if these factors were taken into explicit account.

On future growth in income differentials, it must first be noted that the above computations on both the 1950 and 1960 census figures involved a cross-section "snap-shot." In other words, for each of these census years we know how much a graduate of a given age is earning and by what amount this exceeds the earnings of a typical dropout. Using this sort of information to gauge the financial worth of a current dropout prevention program entails the assumption that the presently young graduate will, as he grows older, be earning more than the also aging dropout by an amount equal to the *present* differential between older graduates and dropouts. This, of course, need not be the case. The difference, in Table 4, between 1949 and 1959 computations of returns indeed suggests that income differentials can grow markedly over time. For several reasons, however, the exact amount of this historical growth is not easy to determine, and predictions about the future can, at present, be performed only by crude extrapolation. There is, of course, no compelling reason why these differentials should

---

[36] Gary S. Becker, *Human Capital* (National Bureau of Economic Research, 1964).

grow at a constant rate, nor is there even any guarantee they will grow at all. Indeed, recent evidence indicates that the income differences between graduates and dropouts actually shrunk between 1957 and 1963.[37]

Despite the uncertainties and some dissident pieces of evidence, most economists commenting on the matter reckon that differentials are likely to be greater in the future. Only Becker, however, has ventured an estimate that can be adopted for our present purposes. His examination of secular income trends leads him to conclude that differentials between dropouts and graduates have been growing at a rate of about 1.25 percent per year.[38] If this is applied to cross-section income streams of the length and shape we have been dealing with, it leads to a returns estimate about 20 percent greater than our original estimates. This in turn would lead to a benefit value that is nearly 90 percent of costs.[39]

The second possible and important adjustment—controlling for ability and other differences between graduates and dropouts—clearly results in a downward correction of returns. There appear to be only two studies that give a hint as to how great this adjustment should be. Both suggest that returns adjusted for ability and other background factors yield a figure that is approximately 70 percent of unadjusted returns.[40] If we accept this figure, it is apparent that the resulting downward adjustment is greater than the upward adjustment due to allowance for growth in income differentials. The combined adjustment suggests that the original figures in Table 4 should be multiplied by 0.84 (the product of 1.2 and 0.7), which means that the "fully" adjusted figures are 84

[37] James Morgan and Charles Lininger, "Education and Income: Comment," *Quarterly Journal of Economics,* Vol. 78, No. 2 (May 1964), pp. 346-47.

[38] *Human Capital,* pp. 73, 124.

[39] Integrating the results of manpower projections into the extrapolation of past trends in differentials could possibly provide an improved estimate of future growth in differentials. No work of this type has yet been tried.

[40] Discussed in Becker, *Human Capital,* pp. 86-88, 125-26. One of the studies involves an analysis of income differences for brothers of differential educational attainments. The other is the study by Morgan and David mentioned in Chap. I (note 18, p. 11). Becker notes that there are reasons for thinking that the former overestimates the independent influence of education and the latter is probably an underestimate. The differences in the two estimates are not, however, very great.

percent of the unadjusted ones. The resulting benefits based on the 1960 census are thereby reduced to less than 60 percent of costs.

The above discussion, aimed at improving Weisbrod's estimates, does not revise essentially his original verdict. Updating the estimates and adjusting for some important neglected factors still leaves benefits considerably short of costs.[41] This is, of course, not the end of the story on the efficiency of dropout prevention programs. More work remains to be done on improving the accuracy of adjustments of the type attempted here. And of even greater importance is the need for more observations. In late 1967 there was only one other (unpublished) case study that attempted to measure the costs of rescuing a potential dropout.[42] Its techniques were patterned after Weisbrod's, and its results indicate an even higher required expenditure per rescue than that discovered in St. Louis. Still more studies are needed so that we can be sure that the observations so far recorded are not atypical. Of the many dropout prevention programs that sprouted in the early 1960's, it is likely at least a few others have kept track of the sorts of data necessary for an adequate benefit-cost study.

It must be cautioned once again, however, that theory and practice have evolved quickly on the matter of treating dropouts and

[41] Since there is a good deal of uncertainty about the assumptions used above, especially those concerning unemployment and the growth of earnings differentials, this result still must be treated with caution. However, the procedures used here for estimating returns are generally no less charitable than the assumptions used in the earlier studies of returns from extra schooling. And on at least two assumptions, the above is more generous than seems warranted. In using the income differences between dropout and graduate females, no adjustment was made for the differences in their labor force participation rates. It can be established that female graduates have a much higher propensity than female dropouts to be in the labor force. Making no special adjustment for this assumes that the implications of voluntary and involuntary unemployment are essentially the same. This probably biases returns upwards (see Weisbrod, "Preventing High School Dropouts," pp. 128-29). Another generous assumption is use of the unadjusted income of youths 16 to 18 years of age as it appears in the census for income foregone. This is generally agreed to be a clear underestimate, though no fully satisfactory alternative has been devised (see Theodore Schultz, "Capital Formation by Education," *Journal of Political Economy*, Vol. 68, No. 6 (December 1960), pp. 573-77; and Becker, *Human Capital*, pp. 171-72).

[42] Arthur J. Corazzini, "Prevention of High School Dropouts: An Analysis of Costs and Benefits," Princeton University, 1965 (mimeo).

potential dropouts. The changes have occurred in two directions. The first is represented by the Neighborhood Youth Corps and the Job Corps, both of which work outside the regular school system. Though a part of these efforts is aimed at encouraging students to return to (or stay in) school, the main thrust is the provision of distinctly nonacademic training for those who, by high school, continue to respond poorly to more traditional types of education. For these sorts of programs, the results of the previous section on retraining are probably more applicable.

The second, and perhaps more basic, change in viewpoint is the notion that underprivileged and poorly performing students should be given special services long before the legal dropout age. Even if the only goal were dropout prevention, most observers seem to feel that this would be a more efficient alternative. But of much greater potential importance is the argument that more intensive education at an earlier age results in more and better learning, dollar for dollar, than does prolongation of education. Chapters 4 and 5 are largely devoted to providing some tests of that proposition.

CHAPTER IV

Compensatory and Preschool Education

As with training programs and dropout campaigns, the start of special efforts to raise the achievement and academic potential of poor children predates the federally sponsored poverty battles. Well publicized programs of this type, supported locally and by foundations, began in some cities during the late 1950's and have since proliferated to hundreds of communities. Elements of the Economic Opportunity Act have been designed to reinforce these projects, and grants under the Elementary and Secondary Education Act of 1965 are being channeled into ongoing programs as well as into new projects.

Compensatory Education

Programs designed to aid school age children are largely a matter of assigning more and better personnel and adding supplementary services to the education of poor children. An additional feature is the attempt to gear instruction to those children's special needs arising from such factors commonly associated with poverty as low educational attainment of parents, large family size, broken homes, discrimination, and slum conditions. "Cultural deprivation" has come to be the key phrase to describe the educational problem posed by these circumstances and "compensatory education" the name for specially designed programs to meet the problem.

The notion of concentrating our efforts in the regular school years has raised many high hopes.[1] And the hopes have been fed by the early reports of success in a number of demonstration projects and model programs.

It is at best questionable, however, whether these first-round projects are truly representative of what large scale, broadly based programs can do to fight poverty. The program that has received the most attention and praise—the Demonstration Guidance Project in New York—would seem to have only limited relevance. This program, like a number of other early efforts, did not seek to affect all children in the school where it took place, but concentrated instead on cultivating the best prospects into college-entrance levels of achievement. While most observers are inclined to rate the program a "success," it is still an open question what this implies for raising the bulk of culturally deprived children up to levels of reasonable achievement.[2]

Making inferences even more risky is the fact that, in the Demonstration Guidance Project, as well as in the other path-breaking efforts, unusual zeal was generated among school personnel. Teachers were easily encouraged to think of themselves as important vanguards. From this, several observers have concluded that high morale was the critical ingredient and have consequently worried that this will not carry over into large, citywide programs.[3]

[1] John Kenneth Galbraith, for instance, has speculated that intensive efforts in slum schools would be "an attack on poverty by what I would judge to be the most effective single step that could be taken" (*Harper's*, Vol. 228, No. 1,366 [March 1964], p. 26).

[2] J. Wayne Wrightstone and others, *Assessment of the Demonstration Guidance Project* (New York Board of Education, 1964). See also Wrightstone and others, "Demonstration Guidance Project in New York City," *Harvard Educational Review*, Vol. 30, No. 3 (Summer 1960), pp. 237-51; and Henry T. Hilson and Florence C. Myers, *The Demonstration Guidance Project, 1957-1962* (New York Board of Education, 1963).

[3] See, for instance, Kenneth B. Clark, *Social and Economic Implications of Integration in the Public Schools*, Seminar on Manpower Policy and Program (U.S. Department of Labor, 1965), p. 21; and Frank Riessman, *The Culturally Deprived Child* (Harper & Row, 1962), pp. 103-05.

For these and other reasons it seems unwise to base benefit-cost studies on the small and intensive efforts that characterized the first stages of the compensatory education movement. Of more apparent relevance are the "second-round" efforts that have been established in several cities. They cover many more students and schools, and their goal usually is to help culturally deprived children of all ability levels. Though the excitement of experimentation still surrounds some of the projects, it is not as predominant as it was in the small earlier programs.

HIGHER HORIZONS PROGRAM

If one were limited to drawing conclusions from a single, large scale compensatory education experiment, the Higher Horizons Program in New York City would have to be the choice. The main reasons for this are the careful controls built into the program, the large number of students observed, and the numerous measures of evaluation. On a technical level, Higher Horizons is far superior to anything attempted elsewhere.

It is also prototypal. Many other cities and communities openly copied the structure and methods of New York's Higher Horizons; some even adopted the name. But though it was one of the first large programs of its kind, it was not New York's first try with compensatory education. Higher Horizons was a direct outgrowth of the Demonstration Guidance Project. Many of the same elements appeared in both programs and some of the lessons of the earlier program were applied in setting up Higher Horizons. It would, therefore, appear to be fairly representative of what can be expected from widely applied compensatory education.

The Higher Horizons program started in 1959 with elementary pupils in the third grade and junior high pupils in the seventh.[4] Special services were inaugurated, including remedial reading, extra counseling of students and parents, cultural activities, and specially tailored curriculum changes—all this backed up by additional teachers and extra professional staff. Pupils in 52 New York elementary schools and 13 junior high schools received these ser-

[4] Descriptive information is from Wrightstone and others, "Evaluation of the Higher Horizons Program for Underprivileged Children," New York Board of Education, 1964 (mimeo).

vices beginning in 1959, and eventually 11 high schools were involved when the initial junior high group reached this level. At its
peak, Higher Horizons' services were being received by 64,075
pupils. The average cost per pupil at all grade levels and through
the duration of the program was approximately $61 per year above
average costs in non-Higher Horizons schools.

To evaluate the effect of the program, pupils in eight of the elementary schools and ten of the junior high schools were closely observed over a three-year time period. Samples of approximately
800 pupils at the elementary level and 1,400 at the junior high
level were used for most types of evaluation. All had remained in
the same Higher Horizons school for at least two years. The main
control group were students in non-Higher Horizons schools (that
is, schools receiving only regular services and costing $61 less per
year per student) who also had remained in the same school for
over two years. They were in the same grade and identical in number to the Higher Horizons sample, and their initial scores on I.Q.
and achievement tests were similar to the sample group both in
central tendency and in variance. The control schools—eight elementary and ten junior high schools—closely resembled the Higher
Horizons schools in size, age of school, and the ethnic and socioeconomic composition of the student body. In short, the only apparent difference between the Higher Horizons group and the control group was the extra $61 worth of services.[5]

The Higher Horizons report includes 141 tables that contain
many different types of information, all of which cannot be adequately covered here. And, for the purpose at hand, much of it has

---

[5] Higher Horizons pupils in junior high schools were also compared, along some
dimensions, with pupils who had entered the same schools slightly earlier, before
Higher Horizons had started. But the meaningfulness of these comparisons is blurred
for at least two reasons. First, because the two groups overlapped to some degree—
that is, were in the same schools though not receiving the same services—the pre-
Higher Horizons pupils may have been given less than usual attention. Second,
since they started school at an earlier date, there is a possibility that the difference
in average expenditures was greater than the $61 that separated the Higher Hori-
zons and the regular control group. How much greater, if at all, cannot easily be
determined. The text, therefore, emphasizes the more readily interpretable results
involving the control groups in other schools. Not much is lost by this emphasis
since comparisons with pre-Higher Horizons students would yield roughly the
same results.

no clear meaning. Measures such as comparative truancy rates and success of peer group relationships have an unclear link with the sorts of predictions that are within our ken of interest. As it turns out, most measures of this sort also have an unclear link with Higher Horizons: few show statistically significant gains in favor of Higher Horizons students.

It would seem that the most meaningful way to sum up the evaluation is to review the sorts of evidence that might suggest that Higher Horizons pupils (1) will continue longer in school, (2) changed their capacity to learn, or (3) actually learned more during the observation period.

1. *Continuation of Schooling.* The Higher Horizons report was prepared before any record was available on how students fared once they reached high school. Thus it contains no direct evidence on whether dropout rates were reduced, let alone whether an increased proportion of students continued their education beyond high school. Still, some parts of the questionnaire answered by the Higher Horizons and control groups give some clue as to what can be expected. The most explicit examples are two questions asked junior high pupils about their academic plans: "Do you expect to go to college or go to work after high school?" and "What type of curriculum do you plan to take in high school (academic, vocational, commercial)?" The small differences that did show up gave contradictory clues: a higher proportion of the Higher Horizons group planned to attend college, but a higher proportion of the control group planned to take the academic curriculum in high school.[6]

Another set of questions, put to elementary and junior high school groups, related to the students' attitudes toward school and school work. Answers to these questions are possibly indicative of the students' chances of at least sticking out high school. The results were again not clearly favorable to the experimental students. The elementary experimental group barely outscored the control group on the attitude index devised by the Higher Horizons research team, and the junior high control group barely outscored their experimental counterparts.[7]

---

[6] Wrightstone and others, "Evaluation of Higher Horizons," pp. 202-03, 209-10.
[7] *Ibid.*, pp. 79-89.

These and similar questions give the distinct impression that Higher Horizons exhibited no tendency toward lengthening educational careers. Until further evidence accumulates, an increase in school continuation cannot be counted as a benefit of Higher Horizons.

2. *Capacity To Learn.* The variability of individual I.Q. scores over time has led many to believe that so-called fixed intelligence can really be manipulated, with specially designed efforts, relatively late in the educational process. Higher Horizons researchers took special care in evaluating the changes in intelligence test scores and analyzed the data in several different ways. The comparison receiving the most attention was the difference in average I.Q.'s, after Higher Horizons had operated for over two years, between Higher Horizons pupils and control groups who had nearly equal I.Q. scores at the beginning of the program. Again, differences between the two groups were small and went in both directions.[8] The thoroughness of this part of the investigation makes it clear that Higher Horizons did not succeed in systematically altering I.Q. scores.

Though Higher Horizons pupils did no better on I.Q. scores than their control counterparts, it is interesting to note that neither group exhibited any systematic decline in scores over the observed time period. This is in sharp contrast with other investigations that show that underprivileged children generally lose I.Q. points as they grow older, especially between eight and eleven years of age. The unusual stability of I.Q. scores over time for pupils in both the experimental and the control group suggests that they experienced more intellectual stimulation than is usually the case with underprivileged children. But a closer look indicates that the stability is more likely attributable to the fact that the only pupils in the final tabulations were those who stayed in the same school for three years. The earlier evidence of apparent decline in I.Q. scores was cross-section evidence and included students from transient families. A high degree of transiency, within the city, but involving changes of school, is a common trait of poor families, and the trait has been associated with poor classroom performance. The Higher Horizons evaluation report therefore con-

[8] *Ibid.*, pp. 37-47, 134-44.

cludes that the stability of the population tested probably led to the stability in test scores.[9] Thus, the stability in test scores, though an intriguing discovery, does not cast serious doubt on the conclusion that Higher Horizons yielded no benefits in terms of increased learning capacity.

3. *Actual Learning.* While altering the I.Q. scores of children in a relatively short time and at a relatively late age may be too much to expect, there is still hope that the same children can absorb more knowledge and attain higher skill levels by way of improved instruction. It would seem that the most objective way to verify this is by scores on standardized achievement tests. The Higher Horizons evaluation relied heavily on such tests, and the controls and exploration of alternative comparisons in these tests were as careful as those for the I.Q. tests. Again, it was a matter of seeing whether Higher Horizons pupils, matched with control groups by test scores at the beginning of the program, differed in performance after approximately two years of special attention. Though Higher Horizons students did not do uniformly better on all such comparisons, their average performance on the composite of test scores indicates that they did learn more at both the elementary and junior high school levels. The differences in gains are expressed in the often-used common denominator of "yearly equivalents." This measure is based on the average achievement scores of pupils, with the same I.Q.'s, who are administered the same test but in different grade levels and fractions of grade levels. Any raw-score gain can thus be translated into the time it normally takes to achieve that gain. In terms of this measure it can be said that pupils in Higher Horizons elementary schools gained 3 percent of a year more in achievement than their control counterparts, and in junior high schools 3.3 percent of a year more.[10]

---

[9] *Ibid.*, pp. 45, 46.

[10] Calculated from data in *ibid.*, pp. 53-55, 64-66, 147-52, 163-65. This represents the average gain on arithmetic achievement and reading achievement tests, for boys and girls. There was no consistent pattern suggesting that either sex tended to gain relatively more from Higher Horizons, nor that either arithmetic or reading was more favorably influenced (relatively) by the program. The straightforward averaging of separate tests, in order to derive an overall level of standardized achievement, is not uncommon. For instance, one testing manual states: "To obtain a measure of general ability which will be a composite of the abilities measured by the subtests in the battery, it is necessary to total or average the scores in some way and then

Since the time between tests for experimental and control groups was identical, the extra gain can be attributed to the greater intensity of the Higher Horizons program.

Was Higher Horizons a success or a failure? The evaluation report ventures no general statements along these lines. It does, however, note that most teachers and principals thought the program had "some positive effects" and that it should be continued. Although the evidence reviewed here seems to verify the "some positive effect" impression of school personnel, it says little about whether gains were substantial *enough* to justify continuance. If the positive effects were costless, there would surely be no question. But they were not costless. (It is unlikely that the added costs were taken into close account by the school personnel who answered the question about continuance.) Of course, no computation can yield an ultimate answer as to whether the results justified the costs. But we can, at least, try to parallel the estimates of Chapter 3 by attempting to place a pecuniary value on the observed gains and see how these compare with costs.

In deriving a pecuniary value from the observed gains there is no body of accepted practice we can turn to. There seems, however, to be only one reasonable way to convert the short-run evi-

---

interpret this average or total in terms of some kind of norms. It is customary to use either the arithmetic mean or the sum of the subtest scores as the value which shall be interpreted in terms of mental age or grade norms" (*Manual for Interpreting Pintner Intermediate Test and Pintner Advance Test* [World Book Company, 1939], p. 7). The manual goes on to note that the median score of separate tests is preferable in cases where there is a worry that the average might be "unduly influenced" by the score on any one test. However, since only two achievement test scores were available for the Higher Horizons experiment, there is no choice but to use the mean of the two. Sometimes more elegant procedures are suggested for deriving a measure of general achievement level (see, for instance, *How to Use the Test Results* [1963 ed.; Science Research Associates], pp. 34-35), but these procedures do not vary substantially from simple averaging of separate tests that are thought to be of comparable importance. The symmetrical treatment in the Higher Horizons evaluation of the two tests suggests that they were in fact considered of equal importance. It might be argued, however, that reading is more basic and therefore more important, in which case a weighted average, favoring reading achievement, would be called for. Given the configuration of test scores in the Higher Horizons experiment, such a weighting would result in a somewhat lower level of overall achievement in elementary school and a somewhat higher level in junior high school.

dence of test scores into later life income. But even this procedure requires some heroic assumptions.

The first necessary assumption is that the gains in yearly equivalents have the same implications for future earnings as do gains in knowledge that result from a continuation of schooling. From Chapter 1 we know that higher achievement, for a given level of school years completed, is associated with higher earnings. But whether years-of-schooling and learning-in-yearly-equivalents have exactly the same earnings effect is not clear from this evidence. For the time being, the two effects are assumed to be identical. With this assumption, the test score gains can be interpreted *as if* Higher Horizons had succeeded in lengthening the educational careers of children. And, since we have some idea of what continuation of schooling means for future earnings, a link is thereby established between test score gains and pecuniary gains.

To make this connection directly, it must also be assumed that the test score gains recorded in the short run will not expand or erode with the passage of time. Either kind of change is very possible. Given the initial thrust of two years of Higher Horizons, the experimental group might pull far ahead of the control group in their rate of later learning. On the other hand, they may slip back to the control group level unless still more money is spent on them all the way through high school. As it turns out, we will never know the final independent impact of the costs observed over those two years because more money *will* be spent on the experimental group. There are, however, at least two reasons to think that the short-term differences would remain at about the same level if no more resources were expended. First, there were no observed alterations in learning capacity as measured by I.Q. scores. Second, the stability of achievement score differences over time has been witnessed in various other longitudinal experiments.[11]

[11] Benjamin S. Bloom, *Stability and Change in Human Characteristics* (Wiley, 1964), Chap. 4. The most relevant experiment was a longitudinal study of reading score changes between grades 2 and 8 (pp. 113-14). The children in this study were divided into two socioeconomic categories, the lower category consisting of children from families where the working head had a high school education or less. When the two groups were ranked by reading scores in the second grade, the top half had an average score of 1.01 yearly equivalents above the lower half. By

Since there seems to be no evidence that argues strongly for either expansion or contraction of the initially observed differences, we can proceed under the assumption of stability.

The final important assumption is that the income differential between high school graduates and dropouts is fairly representative of what (approximately) two years of schooling are worth in economic terms. The analysis of the dropout prevention program in Chapter 3 suggests that, because of various data limitations, this differential is only a rough indication of the true value of not dropping out of high school. Whether it is the best reflection of increased learning for school age children is also open to question. One might choose instead some other differential—say, the lifetime earnings difference between people who have dropped out of high school and those who never went beyond elementary school. But here there is a worry that, at least for younger workers, those with eighth grade education or less are a collection of very atypical individuals. Becker states this view harshly in his comment that "only the physically handicapped, dullards or least-motivated persons fail to go to high school."[12] A related, and perhaps more persuasive, reason why the dropout-graduate differential is more appropriate is that average educational attainment for underprivileged children falls within the tenth to twelfth grade range. If more is learned in earlier years *and* is maintained, it would seem most akin to lengthening the average period in high school, moving it closer to the twelfth grade level. Therefore, the income difference associated with this educational interval seems most suitable for our purposes.

These assumptions are combined with the relevant dollar amounts to yield the benefit-cost figures in Table 5. The basis for computing the financial value for extra learning is the unadjusted

---

the eighth grade, the group in the top half now had an average score of 1.16 yearly equivalents above the group initially in the lower half. While the margin was slightly widened, it must be remembered that the upper half achieved their higher second grade scores without the help of a special program. Thus they were probably more effective learners to begin with. Since there is no evidence that Higher Horizons increased learning capacity along with reading achievement, the longitudinal data from Bloom probably give an optimistic picture of how much better Higher Horizons students will be reading in the future.

[12] *Human Capital*, p. 129.

TABLE 5

Estimates of Benefits and Costs for Higher Horizons Program

Item	Elementary School	Junior High School
1. Present value of one year of extra schooling[a]	$2,410	$2,838
2. Average percent of year gained as result of program[b]	3%	3.3%
3. Benefit per student (line 1×line 2)	$72	$94
4. Number of school years between tests[c]	2.00	1.75
5. Cost per student at $61 per year[d] (line 4×$61)	$122	$107
6. Benefit-cost ratio (line 3÷line 5)	0.59	0.88

[a] Figures based on difference in 1959 mean earnings between graduate and dropout males, white and nonwhite, between the ages of 18 and 65 (see notes d and e, Table 4). No deduction was made for income foregone since there is no presumption that dropout rates are reduced; and cross-sectional differences were not adjusted for ability or for possible growth in differentials. Final values were derived by the following steps: (1) streams of earnings differentials were adjusted for mortality and discounted back to the average age level of children at the start of the program assuming all will enter the labor market at age 18; (2) discounted earnings gain of white and nonwhite females was assumed to be 1.4 times that of their male counterparts (see note e, Table 4); returns were weighted on basis of about as many girls in the program as boys and approximately three-quarters of the pupils nonwhite (Wrightstone and others, "Evaluation of Higher Horizons," pp. 21, 40, 127); (3) discounted and weighted value was halved on assumption that a graduate experiences two years more education than a dropout (see S. M. Miller and others, *The School Dropout Problem* [Syracuse University Youth Development Center, 1963], pp. 11-17; and National Education Association [NEA], *Project School Dropout* [NEA, 1963], p. 3).

[b] Figures are averages for reading and quantitative achievement tests for boys and girls (see text and note 10, pp. 67-68; calculated from data in Wrightstone and others, "Evaluation of Higher Horizons," pp. 53-55, 64-66, 147-52, 163-65).

[c] Slightly more time elapsed between reading tests than between arithmetic tests; the intervals used are averages (from data in *ibid.*, pp. 53, 64, 147, 163).

[d] Cost per year from *ibid.*, p. 4.

difference in lifetime mean earnings as appears in the 1960 census. Since there is no evidence indicating that Higher Horizons students will attend school for a longer period, no deduction was made for income foregone. Thus, the financial value for one extra year of schooling is calculated from earnings differences between graduates and dropouts from age 18 until the assumed retirement

age of 65. Since the average dropout leaves near the end of the
tenth year of school, the earnings difference between graduates
and dropouts was divided by two to derive the value for a single
year of education.

The resulting ratios are not much different from those computed for the dropout prevention program examined in Chapter
3. The financial gains at the elementary school level turn out to be
nearly 60 percent of costs and at the junior high level nearly 90
percent of costs are covered.

It thus appears that the extra costs of compensatory education
exceed the anticipated financial gains. This is, however, the result
of only one observation. While it has been noted that Higher Horizons is the most carefully controlled (and perhaps the most
representative) observation at hand, other programs should be examined before the economic efficiency of compensatory education
can be evaluated.

OTHER PROGRAMS

Though I spent a good deal of time corresponding with and vis-
iting numerous communities with compensatory education programs, I could find none with reports that came near the Higher
Horizons report in comprehensiveness and in the care of experimental design. Many conducted no conscientious research at all.
Among those that did, there was often a reluctance to share their
findings with an outside researcher. Of the few who granted access
to their reports or to school records, some expressed a preference
for anonymity. Hence, the locales of the experiments discussed
here are not disclosed.

Only four programs tabulated standardized test scores for students given special services as well as for students in schools receiving only standard attention. These programs offer the only chance
to associate a given change in performance with the specific influence of compensatory education and the concomitant extra costs.

The four programs are similar in several respects: (1) They
took place in large urban areas outside the deep South. (2) All
four were multischool programs, the smallest involving six experi-

mental schools at the elementary level. (3) Like New York's Higher Horizons, they introduced a number of curriculum changes and special activities along with the addition of new personnel. (4) Each cost somewhat less (per student, per year) than did Higher Horizons.[13]

Three of the programs had one other important thing in common: control groups made slightly greater gains on standardized tests over the period of the experiments than did the children treated to the special compensatory education for over two years.

It cannot, however, be directly concluded from these results that the compensatory education programs were less effective than the standard educational diet. First of all, the difference in mean scores was in no instance close to reasonable levels of statistical significance. Moreover, in all three experiments, the socioeconomic mix of pupils in the control schools was apparently a little higher, which in turn may have accelerated gains for these groups.[14]

This flaw in the experiments had a justification: school administrators were anxious to help the schools with the highest proportion of underprivileged children. From discussions with administrators it was apparent that this understandable wish to aid the neediest schools was not, at the beginning of the program, viewed as a very serious hindrance to the experiment. They anticipated that the experimental schools would still show patently greater improvement. The power of the small socioeconomic differences,

---

[13] Further background information on these programs can be found in App. B.

[14] Only one of the experiments isolated data for pupils who had remained in experimental and control schools for the duration of the experiment. In the other two, pupils in certain grades were tested at the beginning, and two or more years later pupils in the same grades were tested once more. One could then observe if, say, fourth grade scores were higher in the later testing period, and whether increases (if any) were greater in experimental schools than in control schools. One could also observe if the differences between, say, second and fourth grade scores were greater and how they compared in experimental and control schools. An important implication of this technique is that transient students are included in the comparison. Many of the experimental students thus received special services for a short time only. Moreover, as noted earlier, there are strong indications that pupils who move from school to school generally do not perform as well as those who stay in one school. For these reasons alone, then, we might anticipate that these two experiments would not turn out as well as Higher Horizons.

and/or the lack of power of compensatory education programs, came as a surprise.[15]

Despite the ambiguity of the test score comparisons between experimental and control groups, it might still be hoped that other types of evidence could be found that indicate improvement among experimental groups. The available bits of supplementary information are not, however, clearly inconsistent with the control-experimental test score results. Test scores *within* the experimental schools were not markedly higher at the end of the experiment than before its initiation. And the limited information on attitude and aspirational changes also revealed no clearly favorable pattern. Thus, from all the evidence taken together, it must be concluded that there were no palpable, short-run indications that children in these compensatory education programs profited from the experience.[16]

The fourth experiment utilizing control schools presents a happier picture. The children in schools with compensatory education apparently learned more between the early elementary grades and the later ones. There is no longitudinal evidence for this, but only cross-section comparisons made after the program had run for approximately three years. That is, at the end of three years of compensatory education the children who then were in lower and upper grade levels were tested—in both experimental and control schools—and the differential gain over time was inferred from this single snapshot. The yearly equivalent mean scores, second grade compared to fifth grade, were found to be about 7 percent of a year greater for the experimental group. Using the technique of Table 5, this implies an average financial benefit of $168. The program cost $38 extra per year, and therefore $114 for a three-year

---

[15] The difficulty in having a nonidentical socioeconomic mix for experimental and control schools could be surmounted, at least in part, by multiple regression techniques. This would require socioeconomic information for each child in the control and experimental schools, matched with individual test scores. Unfortunately, such information was not collected at the time of the experiments.

[16] Personnel associated with the programs were divided in their interpretation of short-run results. Some felt that subtle and hard-to-measure changes were brought about by the program and that this would likely be verified in tangible performance changes later on. About an equal number saw nothing that controverted the tabulated evidence.

period. Benefits thus appear to exceed costs, the benefit-cost ratio coming out to about 1.5.

The result should, however, be viewed with more than the usual amount of caution. The failure to note longitudinal gains directly is one important worry. The imperfect matching of control and experimental schools is another. The matching in this study did not undertake careful precautions; moreover, the selection of experimental schools was determined, in part, by the receptivity of school principals to the idea of compensatory education. This experiment was also smaller than any of the others discussed here. Only six experimental schools in a very large urban area were involved, and thus a stronger "Hawthorne effect" was likely generated. It is not clear, therefore, that the apparent gains induced by this program can be replicated on a large scale.

One more compensatory education program deserves comment at this point even though the absence of a formal control group disallows comparisons of the sort made above. This program consisted of a summer school for selected underprivileged pupils. The selection was made in terms of attitude, health, and behavior "conducive to participation in the summer school," as well as evidence of "reasonable" ability to learn. Moreover, the pupils were not required by school authorities to attend, but were selected from a group whose parents had already volunteered them for the summer program. Making assessments even more difficult is the fact that the teachers were specially chosen according to their enthusiasm and apparent skill in dealing with underprivileged children.

Tests administered at the beginning and end of the summer classes indicate that approximately one-third of a school year was gained in verbal and quantitative skills. Gains of approximately this size occurred for students in all grade levels involved, from first through sixth. And a follow-up study of a small group of fourth graders who remained in the same school indicated that no erosion of these gains occurred after a year of regular schooling. Nine months after the summer school, the sample of fourth graders was estimated to be still one-third of a year ahead of where they would have been without the summer school.

The financial value of one-third of a school year (calculated in the same way as before) comes out to approximately $700 if discounted back to grade one and a little over $800 if discounted back to grade six. Costs for all grade levels in the eight-week summer program were approximately $160 per pupil. Thus, financial benefits are estimated to be over four times the amount of costs for first graders and range up to nearly six times costs for the sixth grade pupils.

BENEFIT-COST RATIOS

While the past results of compensatory education programs cannot be described as uniformly successful or unsuccessful, the pattern that emerges from the above survey of evidence is not particularly encouraging. For large scale, nonselective programs it appears that the results of New York's Higher Horizons are no worse than average. In two of the five programs in other large urban areas outside the South, financial benefits were estimated to be in excess of costs (see Table 6). But for both programs there is some doubt that this order of success could be repeated for a substantial number of poor children. One lesson that might be drawn from this is that compensatory education is best applied in piecemeal fashion and in circumstances where teachers and children can be encouraged to regard themselves as a select group. More and better observations are needed, however, before this conclusion can be drawn with any confidence.

Another, and perhaps more secure, conclusion is that older children profit no less from compensatory education programs than younger children. In the Higher Horizons program and the summer school experiment, older pupils in the experimental groups recorded academic gains at least as great as those of younger pupils. Since costs were the same for younger and older pupils, and since the discounting of future income gains falls less heavily on the projected earnings of older pupils, calculated benefit-cost ratios are higher for older than for younger pupils. It is important to remember, however, that this outcome depends on the assumption that yearly equivalent gains have the same long-run implication whether they be recorded in relatively early or late stages in the educational process. The wearing away or the snowballing of gains may occur to a significant degree and work against older children.

TABLE 6

Estimates of Benefits and Costs for Compensatory Education Programs in Five Large Urban Areas Outside the South

Item	Program		
	A, B, C	D	E
1. Present value of one year of extra schooling[a]	[b]	$2,308	$2,093-$2,733
2. Average percent of year gained as result of program[c]	[b]	7%	33%
3. Benefit per student (line 1×line 2)	[b]	$162	$690-$902
4. Cost per student[d]	[b]	$114	$160
5. Benefit-cost ratio (line 3÷line 4)	[b]	1.4	4.3-5.6

[a] Calculated by the same method and with the same general assumptions described in note a, Table 5. Values differ somewhat solely because discounting procedure began at different starting points according to age level of children in the program. The younger the children, the longer the wait before they reach working age, and the lower the present value assigned to a given dollar amount of income gain. For program E, a range of values is given since pupils gained from the program as early as the first grade and as late as the sixth.

[b] Benefit-cost ratios were not computed. Experimental groups in these three programs did not make greater gains on standardized tests than did control groups. See App. B for further discussion.

[c] Based on yearly equivalent mean scores of experimental and control groups.

[d] See App. B.

But until such evidence accumulates, it must be concluded that older children should participate no less fully in compensatory education programs than younger children.

It seems apparent that research into the later-life implications of test-score gains, recorded at various levels of schooling, is of prime importance. In the above analysis, the links constructed between test-score gains and future income are not very strong. Yet it is imperative that some short-run measure of gain be employed; otherwise the economic evaluation of educational innovations will have to be postponed for intolerably long periods. The method used above is a stop-gap procedure. Future research should concentrate on the direct relationship between test scores (and other, perhaps more sensitive, indicators) and later academic and economic success. Nonetheless, until such research is accomplished, there seems little recourse but to employ the roundabout procedure devised above.

It can, of course, be agreed that disappointing results should not come as a surprise. There is no reason to believe that *every* experiment will be a success, and much of the compensatory effort is, and for some time will remain, experimental. This, however, argues even more forcefully for the importance of evaluation and of comparison of gains and costs, for just as not every experiment must necessarily fail, so too there can be degrees of success. Labeling a program as compensatory does not insure success, as is clear from the evidence presented. It is therefore imperative that futher evaluations be undertaken.

Preschool Programs

According to many varieties of evidence, learning patterns are firmly fixed before school age.[17] From this it is often concluded that cultural deprivation is most vulnerable to attack in the preschool years. This line of reasoning has found its way into the federal antipoverty effort in the form of Headstart programs for underprivileged children of preschool age.

To evaluate the effects of preschool training, we must once again turn to experiments antecedent to the war on poverty. Only two well controlled observations are available, and even these have not yet recorded actual scholastic attainment for the children in the programs.[18] The latest test data available are I.Q. scores at the end of kindergarten. Both experiments were very small, very intensive, and considerably more costly than a year of standard education or of Headstart training. Hence, they may not truly

[17] See especially Bloom, *Stability and Change;* and the December 1962 Arden House Conference on Pre-School Enrichment of Socially Disadvantaged Children, *Merrill-Palmer Quarterly of Behavior and Development,* Vol. 10, No. 3 (July 1964), pp. 207-309.

[18] From available descriptions of the two programs, little apparent difference existed in either teaching philosophy or program content. Both worked on "personality development and socialization" as well as on language development and general cognitive skills.

represent the effects of massive compensatory education in a non-experimental context.

The first of the programs started with four-year-old slum children whose parents had volunteered them for the special school.[19] This "self-selected" group was then split randomly into experimental and control samples consisting of 41 and 29 students, respectively. The experimental group received one year of intensive nursery school training *and* one year of specially "enriched" kindergarten classes. Two teachers were assigned to classrooms with approximately 20 children, and the latest techniques and equipment were employed. The control group, on the other hand, had no nursery school training, but did go to regular "nonenriched" kindergarten in the second year.

Experimental and control groups were given standardized tests at the start of the nursery school classes and again at the end of kindergarten. At first testing the two groups showed no significant differences in mean scores on two I.Q. tests. At the end of kindergarten the same tests were administered. One revealed a statistically significant difference in favor of the experimental group, the apparent gain amounting to 12 I.Q. points; but the second test resulted in a slightly lower (but statistically insignificant) score for the experimental group as compared to the control group.[20] Since there is no indication that one of these results is more valid than the other, the average of the two—6 I.Q. points—seems to be the fairest statement of gain.[21]

Assessing the economic value of I.Q. gains is only a little more perilous than what has been attempted up to now. The first necessary step is to assume that the "artificially" increased I.Q. scores will not fade or grow still greater over time. No evidence exists on

[19] Leo S. Goldstein, "Evaluation of an Enrichment Program for Socially Disadvantaged Children," New York Medical College, Institute for Developmental Studies, June 1965 (mimeo). The program took place in selected Harlem schools; the observations discussed in the text were recorded during the period 1962-64.

[20] *Ibid.*, App. Tables 5 and 18. The test showing the 12 point difference was the Stanford-Binet Intelligence Scale, and the test showing no significant difference was the Columbia Mental Maturity Scale.

[21] This procedure is consistent with that of the compensatory schooling programs where the test-score gains, used in the final calculations, consisted of averages for separate tests judged to be of equal importance and validity. See note 10, p. 67.

this particular point, though it might be noted that I.Q. scores in early childhood (under normal circumstances) have respectable correlations with I.Q.'s in late adolescence.[22] Supposing that the average I.Q. differential observed in the kindergarten test does hold steady and is a reliable prediction of later I.Q., it must then be asked what improvement in academic achievement is associated with this higher I.Q. score.

A recent study on such relationships suggests that 6 points of higher I.Q. (in the relevant range) normally means about 0.7 of a year of extra achievement.[23] As an approximation of the later-life income implication of this gain, the procedure used in the section on compensatory education can be applied here. Discounting to age 4 the estimated value of 0.7 year of schooling (mean earnings basis) yields a value of $1,395.[24] Expenditures per pupil for the nursery and kindergarten program are in excess of this figure. They were approximately $2,800 for the two years together; subtracting $400 to take account of the regular kindergarten services received by the control group yields a net cost of $2,400.[25] Financial benefits divided by costs results in a 0.58 ratio.[26]

A second preschool experiment was, in several ways, similar to the one just discussed. Yearly expenditures per pupil were about the same, children were self-selected from the same sort of socio-

[22] Bloom (*Stability and Change*, p. 61) concludes that the correlation between I.Q. scores at ages 4 and 17 is approximately .80.

[23] "Test Data Reports," Nos. 1-44, Test Department of Harcourt, Brace and World, 1964 (mimeo). The calculation in the text was derived from Reports 3, 18, and 28. Based on nationwide samples of children, these reports list the expected scores for the Stanford Achievement and the Metropolitan Achievement tests which are associated with scores on the Otis Quick-Scoring Ability Test and the Pintner General Ability Test. I.Q. and achievement tests were taken in the same grade by students in grades 4 through 9. All grade levels show roughly the same relationship between I.Q. points and yearly equivalent achievement; most correlation coefficients are close to .70.

[24] Calculated from the same basic data and with the assumptions used in Tables 5 and 6. These procedures yield a value of $1,992 for one year of schooling discounted back to age 4.

[25] Estimated from budget data at the Institute for Developmental Studies, New York Medical College.

[26] If we used only the results from the test indicating a 12 point gain, for the experimental group, and kept all other assumptions the same, it is apparent that estimated financial benefits would be doubled. This would leave us with a $2,790 benefit estimate and a benefit-cost ratio of 1.16.

economic population, and tests were administered to control and experimental groups at the beginning of nursery school and at the end of kindergarten.[27] Two essential differences should, however, be noted. First of all, both the experimental and control groups were limited to children of unusually low I.Q.'s. No mental defectives were included but, rather, only children who were judged to be suffering from severe cultural deprivation. A second difference was that the experimental groups attended kindergarten classes of the usual "nonenriched" sort, similar to those attended by the control group.

At the start of the experiment and at the end of kindergarten no significant differences showed up in the mean scores on a wide variety of intelligence tests. Significant differences did appear at the beginning of kindergarten, but one year of identical kindergarten treatment for both groups apparently erased these gains. At this last testing, scores on the diverse battery of tests reveal the same statistically insignificant differences that appeared at the start of nursery school.[28]

The available evidence on the efficacy of preschool training thus seems no more encouraging than the more abundant compensatory education evidence. As with the conclusions from the preceding analyses, this result must be heavily qualified with the reminder that the observations are not necessarily representative of what new programs will yield and that the technique used to project income gains is far from ideal. With this in mind, about all that can

[27] David E. Weikert and others, "Perry Preschool Project Progress Report," Ypsilanti, Michigan, Public Schools, June 1964 (mimeo). All children resided in the Perry School district in Ypsilanti. The experiment was divided into three "waves," with the total experimental group numbering 36 and the control group numbering 38. The results reported in the text refer only to the first wave with an experimental group of only 13 and a control group of 15 (*ibid.*, p. 5). Cost figures were obtained from personal correspondence.

[28] *Ibid.*, pp. 28-42. Included among the tests were the Stanford-Binet Intelligence Scale, Leiter International Performance Scale, Peabody Picture Vocabulary Test, Illinois Test of Psycholinguistic Abilities, and Gates Reading Readiness Test. A second wave of control and experimental children is still to be evaluated at the end of kindergarten. The experimental group in this wave had two years of nursery school rather than one, and perhaps this will produce a perceptible and lasting difference in their favor. Appreciable differences showed up at the end of one year of nursery school, but by the beginning of kindergarten the difference was smaller, at this stage, than it was for the first wave of the experiment.

be said is that available evidence does not permit the claim that preschool programs by themselves have greater antipoverty leverage than other sorts of education and training programs. Longer-run evidence from follow-up studies may prove differently. Among other things, it might be speculated that preschool programs brought about subtle but basic changes that will lead to longer school continuation. But for that we can only wait and see.

CHAPTER V

Increased Per-Pupil Expenditures

In the two preceding chapters we have considered the effectiveness of very brief spurts of extra educational efforts. The programs reviewed have entailed no more than three years and as little as a few weeks of special schooling. All have been attempts at a big leap forward and were undertaken with the hope that the distance gained would not be lost with the passage of time. And, with the exception of the job retraining programs, all involved to some degree an unnatural experimental atmosphere. To help put these programs in perspective, this chapter considers the effect of increased educational expenditures over the entire span of regular school years.

The analysis here is based on cross-section data tabulated in the recent past. It does not single out schools and school districts that employ special techniques currently thought to be the most effective in teaching underprivileged children. Pupils of low socioeconomic status are simply categorized according to the expensiveness of the schools they have attended. The relationship between expenses and several measures of individual achievement recorded in advanced stages of schooling is thus noted. This relationship does not, of course, depict the best possible academic outcomes that can be generated with additional educational resources. However, the Elementary and Secondary Education Act of 1965 does not require that recipient school districts use funds in optimal fashion. And it is not unlikely that the simple cross-sectional relationship between expenditures per pupil and academic performance may be a fair

83

statement of the academic gains resulting from this act.[1] Even if this is not the case, the analysis here at least provides a "check" on our earlier calculations on compensatory education programs.

Project Talent

For the purposes of this chapter, the richest and most comprehensive source of available data is a statistical survey called Project Talent.[2] It covers 5 percent of all high schools and high school students in the contiguous United States. One of its basic aims is to associate the degree of career success of former pupils with the characteristics of the high school attended. One of these variables is the focus of the present section: expenditures per pupil. The study is still in progress, and it will be several years before we know how close the relationship truly is between expenditures per pupil and future economic success. In the meantime, a number of short-run indications, similar to the output measures considered in Chapters 3 and 4, are available.

Two large volumes on interrelationships have already been published from this survey,[3] and since the appearance of these volumes, some especially useful types of information have been accumulated and organized by Project Talent. Perhaps the most interesting unpublished data is on the socioeconomic status of pupils in

[1] The 1965 education act does specify that payments are to be used for "programs and projects . . . which are designed to meet the special educational need of educationally deprived children" (Title I, Sec. 205). This doubtlessly resulted in curriculum changes (hopefully for the good) as well as in an increase in expenditures per child; and to the extent this was the case the results of the earlier section on compensatory education may be more relevant. Nonetheless, it should be noted that some (and perhaps a majority) of affected school districts already had special programs before the passage of this legislation.

[2] For a description, see John C. Flanagan and others, *Designing the Study*, Technical Report to U.S. Office of Education, Cooperative Research Project 566 (University of Pittsburgh, Project Talent Office, 1960).

[3] Flanagan and others, *Studies of the American High School*, Technical Report to U.S. Office of Education, Cooperative Research Project 226 (University of Pittsburgh, Project Talent Office, 1962); and Flanagan and others, *The American High School Student*, Technical Report to U.S. Office of Education, Cooperative Research Project 635 (University of Pittsburgh, Project Talent Office, 1964).

the Project Talent sample. To derive a status measure, each student was asked nine questions that ranged from father's occupation, income, and education to the number of electrical appliances in the home. These were distilled into a single index number making it possible to compare similar individuals in high schools throughout the country. It also allows the identification of that group of youths, nationwide, who are lowest on the ladder in terms of economic well-being and cultural deprivation.

Also newly tabulated are the results of a mail questionnaire survey of individuals one year beyond the time they should have graduated from high school who were in the ninth grade during the *initial* Project Talent survey. With this information we can calculate, for youths of low socioeconomic status, the percent who fail to complete high school once having started and also the proportion of pupils who immediately go on to college or some other type of post-secondary education. To complement the school continuation data, scores on standardized achievement tests are available, again for pupils of low socioeconomic status.

As an approximation of what the effects of increased expenditures on poor children will be, let us first consider all male pupils who ranked nationally in the bottom 20 percent according to the Project Talent socioeconomic index. They can be identified according to school district, and each school district can be identified according to expenditures per pupil. We can then witness how low socioeconomic class pupils, in school districts of given costs, perform on the standardized tests and how long they typically continue their schooling.

Table 7 shows these relationships for pupils in the general high schools sample in the Project Talent survey. Average scores for two batteries of standardized tests are tabulated here. The first ("academic aptitude") emphasizes proficiency in basic verbal and mathematical skills; the second ("non-academic technical") is a gauge of mechanical, electrical, and scientific information the individual has at hand. Scores at the twelfth grade level are used in order to pick up the "full" effect of the increased expenditures. They have been converted into yearly equivalents according to the average raw scores recorded for all students in grades nine through twelve.

TABLE 7

Test Scores and School Continuation, by Expenditure Categories, for Low Status Boys in Project Talent Survey

School District Expenditure Per Pupil	Number of Low Status Boys[a]	Mean Test Score		Percent Not Completing High School	Percent Terminating at High School Graduation[d]	Percent Enrolled in Junior or Senior College	Percent Enrolled in Other Post-Secondary Education[e]
		Academic Aptitude Test[b]	Non-academic Technical Test[c]				
Less than $200	845	8.73	8.34	14.0	37.9	26.7	21.4
$200-$300	1,552	9.85	9.35	16.1	30.2	31.1	22.6
$300-$400	1,910	10.10	9.93	14.3	29.5	30.6	25.6
$400-$500	1,168	10.21	10.38	17.8	29.0	28.3	25.0
$500 and over	828	10.25	10.26	16.8	23.8	35.6	23.8
All districts	6,303	9.91	9.71	15.7	30.1	30.3	23.9

Source: University of Pittsburgh, Project Talent Data Bank, a National Data Bank for Research in Education and the Behavioral Sciences.

[a] Number and test score information refer to all low status boys, in the twelfth grade of general high schools, who took the battery of Project Talent tests in the spring of 1960. Data on school continuation are from mail questionnaires sent to pupils who were in the ninth grade in the spring of 1960 (number and distribution of low status ninth grade boys by expenditure category is approximately the same as for twelfth grade boys); response rate on the questionnaires was less than 50 percent, and only 2,850 responses were usable.

[b] Based on weighted average of separate tests covering mathematical information, mathematical problem solving, English usage, vocabulary, reading comprehension, abstract reasoning, and creativity. Raw scores were converted into yearly equivalents by observing the mean raw score for all boys in various grade levels and then interpolating. Extrapolation was necessary to derive a yearly equivalent estimate for low status boys in the lowest cost category.

[c] Based on weighted average of separate tests covering mechanical, electrical, aerospace, physical science, and bioscientific information. Yearly equivalents were calculated as described in note b.

[d] Individuals were surveyed less than a year after their scheduled graduation. Figures do not account for possibility some may attend college or other post-secondary school later in life. It was assumed that individuals still in high school, presumably as a result of failure to be promoted, would soon graduate but would not continue their schooling.

[e] Includes "business school, trade school, and armed forces enlisted school."

Perhaps the most striking result of the test score evidence is the very low marks attained by low status boys in school districts of all expenditure levels. Regardless of the expensiveness of education, the mean score for low status boys in the twelfth grade is consistently less than 11—the mean score for all *eleventh* grade boys taking the Project Talent tests. Even so, it seems clear that low status boys in higher expenditure schools do accumulate more knowledge than their counterparts in low expenditure schools. The effect of increased school expenditures on test performance is shown to be the strongest at the lower end of the expenditure range. A difference of more than a full year of achievement appears between boys in school districts spending less than $200 and districts spending between $200 and $300. The apparent power of increased expenditures to improve performance diminishes progressively with each successive expenditure level.

The school continuation data present a picture that is not so neat. The relationship between expenditures and the percent not completing high school is uneven and, by and large, goes in the "wrong" direction: dropout rates tend to be higher in school districts with higher expenditures. The tabulation on the percent enrolled in junior or senior college and in other types of post-secondary education is only a little more encouraging. Moving from the lowest to the next-to-lowest expenditure category, the percentage rises for both types of school continuance. At higher levels of expenditures, however, the direction of the relationship is ambiguous.

Table 8 provides the same sort of tabulations at a lower level of aggregation. All schools in cities over 250,000 are excluded and the remaining sample is split into South and non-South subsamples. Again, the only students considered are those who rank nationally in the bottom 20 percent on the socioeconomic index.

Large cities were excluded because the Project Talent data tapes did not identify cities according to region. Furthermore, complete cost figures were available only by school districts, presenting the problem that most low status students in a high expenditure city might be crowded into slum schools that are a good deal lower in quality than the city average.[4] It is not possible to determine to what degree this might be true or how this might vary from city to city. Thus, while exclusion of the large cities leaves out an important part of the current policy problem, it was

[4] Patricia Sexton, *Education and Income* (Viking Press, 1961), presents copious documentation that schools attended by predominantly low status students, in at least one large midwestern city, receive less educational services of nearly every variety than the city average.

TABLE 8

Test Scores and School Continuation, by Expenditure Categories,
for Low Status Boys in Project Talent Survey in Communities
of Less Than 250,000 Population

School District Expenditure Per Pupil	Number of Low Status Boys	Mean Test Score		Percent Not Completing High School	Percent Terminating at High School Graduation	Percent Enrolled in Junior or Senior College	Percent Enrolled in Other Post-Secondary Education
		Academic Aptitude Test	Non-academic Technical Test				
		North and West					
Less than $200	99	9.64	10.00	*12.3*	*29.8*	*28.1*	*29.8*
$200-$300	473	10.23	10.27	*14.1*	*31.3*	*31.0*	*23.6*
$300-$400	1,512	10.31	10.32	*13.4*	*30.3*	*30.5*	*25.8*
$400-$500	903	10.38	10.67	*14.8*	*31.2*	*28.9*	*25.0*
$500 and over	602	10.26	10.63	*19.4*	*23.9*	*32.8*	*23.9*
All districts	3,589	10.29	10.45	*14.7*	*29.7*	*30.5*	*25.1*
		South					
Less than $200	746	8.61	8.11	*14.3*	*39.1*	*26.4*	*20.1*
$200-$300	927	9.46	8.52	*17.8*	*32.6*	*28.3*	*21.2*
$300-$400	101	9.27	8.01	*19.3*	*43.9*	*35.1*	*1.8*
$400-$500	—	—	—	—	—	—	—
$500 and over	—	—	—	—	—	—	—
All districts	1,774	9.09	8.32	*16.2*	*36.2*	*28.3*	*19.4*

Source: Project Talent Data Bank; calculations are the same as those described in notes of Table 7.

the only means of isolating more homogeneous and meaningful samples.

This less aggregated picture alters our first impression only slightly. There is still a tendency for higher test scores to be associated with higher expenditure levels, and there still appears to be a bigger expenditure effect on scores at the lower expenditure levels. Overall, the test score differences are slightly smaller between expenditure levels than in the more aggregated tabulations. The school continuation relationships also do not differ markedly from those of Table 7. The perverse association between expenditures and dropout rates still occurs, and it appears stronger and more consistent than in the aggregated tabulations. On college attendance, the shape of the relationship in the North and West subsample is similar to that in the aggregated numbers. For the South taken alone, this association is more consistently favorable. The figures on post-secondary training other than college reveal no clear and particularly interesting pattern.

For numerous reasons the above tabulations may not represent the actual effect on academic outcomes of adding resources to schools attended by poor children. However, the most worrisome sources of bias at least seem to have the convenient property of working in the same direction: nearly all appear to bias the results upwards. Before attempting to distill a benefit-cost estimate from Tables 7 and 8, some of the possible sources of distortion should first be noted.

Perhaps the most serious flaw in the tabulations is the imperfect control for socioeconomic status. There is considerable and well-known evidence indicating that differences in family background are critical determinants of educational outcomes; and while Tables 7 and 8 deal exclusively with the bottom socioeconomic quintile, there is reason to think that this control is insufficient. This is because higher cost schools are populated by students of higher average socioeconomic class.[5] From this it can be inferred that low status pupils (as defined above) in high cost schools are likely to be of higher status than low status pupils in relatively low cost schools. Thus, the pupils in high cost schools would likely have better academic records even without the more expensive training; and, it would follow, adding resources in the lower cost schools would result in lower academic outcomes than is indicated by the outcomes recorded in schools with higher present costs.

Related to this is the likelihood that the higher average socioeco-

---

[5] For a recent study finding positive correlations between socioeconomic variables and spending on education among communities, see Jerry Miner, *Social and Economic Factors in Spending for Public Education* (Syracuse University Press, 1963), Chap. 5. Published figures from Project Talent show similar correlations between the average socioeconomic status of communities and expenditures per child. See the analysis in Flanagan and others, *Studies of the American High School*, Chap. 9.

nomic status of pupils in relatively high cost schools resulted in higher aspirations among lower status students, a better atmosphere for learning, and an ability on the part of the school district to obtain superior teachers without paying high premiums. If this is in fact the case, it is an additional reason why injecting added funds into presently low cost districts would not result in outcomes as high as those observed in districts with relatively high expenditures.

It is possible, however, that the higher socioeconomic milieu of the high cost districts also has a negative effect on the morale of low status pupils. It is possible as well that, since low status pupils in high cost districts are a small socioeconomic minority, their special educational needs are not served very efficiently. Both of these phenomena would tend to bias our results downwards. Unfortunately, no direct evidence is available (to my knowledge) as to the prevalence and relative quantitative effects of these possibilities.

Another possible source of bias is the indiscriminate lumping together of all schools in communities of less than 250,000 population. As argued above, eliminating the large cities from the analysis brings us closer to a more homogeneous and more meaningful sample. But it is possible to construct narrower population categories, and analyzing these separately or as dummy variables would likely yield still more meaningful estimates. Nevertheless, from a recent detailed study of school districts in New York state,[6] it appears that the failure to analyze narrower categories of communities also leads to an overoptimistic estimate of the effect of higher expenditures. Like the above tabulations, the New York study examines cross-section data in order to determine the association between expenditures and test scores. It controls for socioeconomic class, as well as several other variables, and computes numerous regression estimates with alternative assumptions. One of its most interesting findings is that the regression coefficients (relating dollars to test scores) for narrower population categories—rural, small-town, urban, and large city—are all smaller than the coefficients derived when all districts are considered together.[7]

[6] Herbert J. Kiesling, "Measuring a Local Government Service: A Study of Efficiency of School Districts in New York State" (unpublished doctoral dissertation, Harvard University, 1965).

[7] *Ibid.*, pp. 34-38, 76-82. Generally this study indicates a smaller impact of dollars

Finally, it should be noted that even if "all" observable interfering variables could be statistically controlled so that one could compare communities that were apparently identical—except for expenditures per pupil—the question arises as to why one school district spent more than another. The most immediate answer that comes to mind is that, for reasons undetected in the observed variables, the citizens in the lower expenditure community have a relatively lower regard for education. It seems reasonable that the children in the community would share these sympathies so that, if the low expenditure district is subsidized from the outside to match the currently high expenditure district in terms of per pupil costs, it could be anticipated that school outcomes still would not be as favorable as they presently are in the high expenditure district. Thus, an additional reason is present for thinking that cross-section comparisons exaggerate the favorable effect of providing more educational resources for poor children.

Benefit-Cost Estimates

Turning now to the calculation of a benefit-cost estimate, it seems clear that the North and West subsample is the best basis for an approximation. Over half of the pupils in the total Project Talent sample are in this subgroup. Moreover, this subgroup should yield more reliable answers than the other possible bases. It avoids the problems of large cities inherent in the total sample. And the failure to control for race is not as great a worry as it is for the South subsample.[8]

In calculating the benefits accompanying higher educational outlays, Tables 7 and 8 make it difficult to justify the inclusion of

---

on test score results than is suggested by Tables 7 and 8. The most influential reason for this seems to be the control for I.Q. scores of pupils which was injected into all computations. It could be argued this is an overly stringent procedure since the presumably superior education in relatively expensive schools could have had as one of its effects the raising of I.Q. scores.

[8] The Project Talent survey *did not* collect information on race. See James S. Coleman and others, *Equality of Educational Opportunity* (U.S. Office of Education, 1966); this survey is especially useful in permitting more analyses of Southern school districts.

longer education as a net gain. The tendency for high school dropout rates to rise with expenditures is at least as strong as the tendency for rates of post-secondary school attendance to rise along
with expenditures.[9] And since the present focus is on alleviating
poverty, the former tendency should be of greater importance in
our assessments than is the latter. (In terms of the framework of
Chapter 2, the income changes associated with dropping out of
high school occur in ranges where dollars should be weighted
more heavily as compared to income changes associated with education beyond high school.) Thus, it appears that we are once
again compelled to rely exclusively on the yearly equivalent
change in test scores as a means for estimating financial benefits.

To make such an estimate, let us suppose that the test score
gains from this can be fairly approximated by the difference in
mean test scores between the expenditure category the pupils are
now in and the category immediately higher. Continuing the strat-
egy of being charitable in our estimates, only the bottom three expenditure categories will be considered. (It will be recalled that
the test scores in the fourth expenditure category were higher than
those in the top category.) Table 9 provides a distillation of the
relevant data in Table 8. The differences in test score averages between expenditure categories appear beside the category that is
moved upward by that amount. The simple differences for the "academic" and "nonacademic" tests are first averaged together and
then adjusted to take account of the fact that the differences in
mean expenditures between categories are not exactly $100. The
final column indicates the yearly equivalent test score gain esti-

[9] The reason why high school dropout rates are higher in relatively expensive
school districts is a riddle that cannot be resolved completely at this time. It may
be due to the sampling error involved in the low response on the mail questionnaire, or it may be that more pupils in the relatively low expenditure districts
leave school before ninth grade. A more interesting speculation is that low status
pupils in the relatively high cost districts split into two groups that react very
differently to the pressures of attending school with predominantly high status
populations: they either adopt the value systems of the majority and attempt to
compete academically, or they experience a strong feeling of alienation and dis-
couragement, possibly more intense than if the bulk of their classmates were of
the same socioeconomic status. Such a dichotomy in behavior patterns would help
explain why the rate of college attendance is higher in the expensive school districts,
even though the dropout rate is also relatively high.

TABLE 9

Estimated Gains in Test Scores in Table 8 Resulting from a $100 Change in Expenditures, North and West Subsample[a]

School District Expenditure Per Pupil	Number of Low Status Boys	Average Change in Test Scores by Moving to Next Expenditure Category[b]	Difference in Mean Expenditures Between Categories	Average Change in Test Scores Associated with $100 Change in Expenditures (yearly equivalent)[c]
	(1)	(2)	(3)	(4)
Less than $200	99	0.43	`$145	0.30
$200-$300	473	0.07	83	0.08
$300-$400	1,512	0.20	92	0.22
All districts	2,084	—	—	0.19[d]

[a] The sample, the expenditure categories, and the number of boys are defined in Table 8.
[b] Average of "academic" and "nonacademic" tests expressed in yearly equivalents in Table 8.
[c] Column 2 $\times$ ($100 $\div$ Column 3).
[d] Weighted average with weights based on number of boys in each category.

mated to occur as a result of an increment of $100 in expenditures.

The estimate of what this $100 does for the "typical" poor child should, of course, be a weighted average of the gains in each category. This weighting is performed according to the number of boys in each category. The resulting average is 0.19 yearly equivalents.

In computing the present value of the financial gain associated with this test score increase, it must be remembered that the cost data are tabulated by school districts. This implies that pupils in higher expenditure categories enjoyed higher quality education through their entire public school careers and not only during the four years of high school. There is no good reason for thinking that any one of these years of higher quality is less important than any other in enabling the pupil to accumulate more learning. All twelve years are, therefore, considered inseparable for the purposes of the analysis. This in turn suggests that the discounting should begin with the first year of education. Discounting accordingly, using the same earnings basis as in Chapter 4 and assuming that all individuals enter the labor force at age 18, the present financial value of 0.19 yearly equivalents is $417.

Costs must also be discounted back to the first grade level. It would be clearly wrong, however, to assume that a difference of $100 prevailed in each of the twelve years of education. Educational expenditures are usually lower in the earlier grades than in later ones; in other words, school districts that differ by $100 can be shown to differ by less than that at the early grade levels and more than that at the upper levels. Application of the discounting formula, which weights earlier costs more heavily, would therefore give an upward bias to discounted costs if allocations by level are ignored. Though we do not know how individual districts in the samples allocated their costs, the typical distribution of expenditures by grade level can be inferred from other statistical sources, and reasonable adjustments can be made.[10] A second problem cannot be resolved so neatly because of an absence of historical cost data on the sample school districts. Cost differentials are known for only the year of the survey, and they may not be entirely representative of the differential existing when the present crop of twelfth graders were in elementary school and junior high. To account for the likely shifts in differentials through time, a crude adjustment was made on the basis of per pupil expenditures by states.[11]

[10] A cost survey conducted by the Office of Education, at approximately the time that the Project Talent cost information was gathered, indicates that per pupil costs at the junior high school level are roughly 75 percent of those at the high school level, and elementary school costs about 70 percent. The $100 increment relevant to the analysis in the text was apportioned accordingly. (U.S. Department of Health, Education, and Welfare, *Current Expenditures per Pupil in Public School Systems: Urban School Systems, 1958-59*, Circular No. 645 [1961], Table 6.)

[11] The states were divided into two groups: those spending more than the average amount per pupil in 1959-60, and those spending less. The average cost for each group was then calculated. Average costs for the same two groups were also examined for 1947-48. The differential in 1947-48 costs between low cost and high cost states (as ranked in the 1959-60 period) proved to be about 60 percent of the differential calculated in the later period, in terms of constant dollars. Thus, costs in the first grade (after adjustment for the distribution of costs by school level, as described in note 10) were multiplied by 0.60; and costs between the first and eleventh grade were multiplied by larger fractions according to linear interpolation

TABLE 10

Estimates of Benefits Derived from Additional Educational Expenditures of $100 per Student per Year

Item	Amount
1. Present value of one year of schooling[a]	$2,196
2. Average percent of year gained as result of $100 increase[b]	19%
3. Benefit per student (line 1 × line 2 ÷ 100)	$417
4. Cost per student for 12 years (unadjusted and undiscounted)	$1,200
5. Cost per student for 12 years adjusted and discounted to first grade[c]	$749
6. Benefit-cost ratio (line 3 ÷ line 5)	0.56

[a] Value discounted to first grade.
[b] See Table 9, column 4.
[c] Adjusted for variability of educational costs by level of education and for secular shifts in educational costs among school districts (see text and notes, pp. 93-94).

Making these adjustments and discounting the cost stream back to first grade results in a $749 total cost figure for all twelve grades associated with a current differential of $100 per year.[12] The resulting benefit-cost ratio is equal to 0.56 (see Table 10). Adding ex-

between 0.60 and the full weight given to costs in twelfth grade. (Cost figure taken from U.S. Department of Health, Education, and Welfare, Office of Education, *Biennial Survey of Education, 1950-60* [1964], Chap. 2, Table 43.)

[12] Among other possibly important considerations omitted is fixed plant and equipment. The questions concerning costs put to school superintendents did not include a request for dollar value of the physical plant or for depreciation changes or imputed interest and rent. Comparing the cost figures used in the above calculations with U.S. government cost surveys of the same period, it is apparent that most (if not all) of the superintendents excluded capital changes from their estimates of cost. And since it is likely that capital costs vary directly with current costs, this exclusion tends to overstate the amount of educational gain brought about by an expenditure increase. To produce the sorts of gains associated with the $100 increase tabulated above, it is likely that additional amounts would have to be spent on improving plant and equipment. This imperfection in our estimates tends to bias benefit-cost ratios upwards.

A second oversight, which tends to have the opposite effect, is our failure to take into account the effects of pupil mobility. Some of the pupils in high cost districts in the twelfth grade of schooling surely spent some of their earlier years in lower cost schools, and vice versa. These movements tend to narrow the observed differential in achievement associated with $100 in present costs. Unfortunately, the quantitative importance of this problem, as compared to the problem of neglecting capital costs, is not commensurable at this time.

penditures through all grades of public schooling thus appears no more effective, dollar for dollar, than short bursts of educational effort of the kind analyzed in Chapter 4.

One final comment is called for at this point on the workings of the Elementary and Secondary Education Act of 1965. Title I of that act, which contains the major provisions concerning poor children, specifies that expenditure allocations to school districts be proportioned according to the amount currently being spent per child in the respective state. That is to say, poor children in states already spending appreciable amounts on education will benefit from a higher dollar increase in educational expenditures than children in low expenditure states.[13] The computations in Tables 7 and 8 give little economic support for this allocation formula. Indeed, these tables suggest that higher dollar returns, per dollar spent, would occur in communities now spending relatively little money on education. Corroborating this is the New York state study, where the effects of added expenditures appeared more potent in the lower expenditure range.[14]

Payoffs of the Various Education Programs

The main task of Chapters 3, 4, and 5 was to arrive at a judgment about what types of educational change yield the most favorable payoff rates. The paucity of observations and the conceptual and measurement difficulties encountered, and only partially resolved,

[13] The formula for distributing funds under Title I is expressed as follows: $a/2 \times b =$ number of dollars payable to local school district, where $a =$ average expenditure per pupil in the state, and $b =$ number of children age 5 to 17 coming from families with annual incomes of less than $2,000 and number of children age 5 to 17 from families whose incomes from Aid to Families with Dependent Children are $2,000 or more. (*Elementary and Secondary Education Act of 1965*, S. Rept. 146, 89 Cong. 1 sess. [April 1965], p. 6.)

[14] Kiesling, "Measuring a Local Government Service," Chap. 3. Kiesling experiments with linear fits as well as with several curvilinear forms. In the several different regressions performed with various subsamples and for test scores in various grade levels, a logarithmic function more closely fits the data in over half the cases. In one interesting case, the closest fit was obtained by a quadratic function, indicating that test scores rose with expenditures through the low ranges of expenditure categories and then fell at the higher ranges.

during the course of calculating benefit-cost ratios make it clear that for the present this judgment can only be very tentative. Nevertheless, three conclusions seem worthy of stress.

1. Vocationally oriented training, at least in the form of recent manpower training programs, exhibits a higher rate of payoff than does general education. The rates are sufficiently in excess of those computed for improvements in general education that it is difficult to dismiss this result as an accident due entirely to the particular estimating techniques used. It should be noted also that job training would likely appear an even more favorable option if a weighted benefit-cost estimate were performed similar to that suggested in Chapter 2. This is so because, in the case of job training, there is not as much guesswork involved in concentrating the educational effort on those who will likely have low incomes in the future. Of the poor children who are still in the public schools, many will do well as adults independently of an extra educational thrust at this time. For those who are in (or about to enter) the labor market, the signs of future income difficulties are more clear-cut. It is also likely that the dispersion in income gains associated with improved general education is likely to be greater than in the case of job retraining. Thus, even if the average payoff rates were identical for general education and job training, we could anticipate that a larger proportion of the individual gains from job retraining would take place in the income ranges that are of greatest concern in a war on poverty.

It should come as no great surprise that an extension of vocational training brings about a higher average amount of economic success, per dollar spent, than does general education. That, after all, is its nearly exclusive aim. General education, on the other hand, is normally expected to yield a rich assortment of direct and indirect benefits in addition to that of simply raising incomes. These anticipated benefits should be kept in mind when it comes to final policy decisions; that is, the apparent superiority of vocational training as an antipoverty weapon must surely be tempered by the consideration that general education may be preferable on other counts. Much of the discussion in Chapter 6 is directly relevant to this issue.

2. The payoff-rate evidence gives no strong indications that spe-

cial emphasis should be placed on the very early school years or on the preschool years. Contrary to most current opinion, "the younger the better" is not an unassailable maxim. In the two compensatory education programs that recorded outcomes at different grade levels, children in the upper levels appeared to have gained at least as much, dollar for dollar, as did children in the lower grade levels. And the preschool programs observed did not clearly indicate that payoff rates here are any higher than they are for educational improvements in the school years. Thinking again in terms of a weighted benefit-cost estimate (which counts as more important the gains received by poorer individuals) this conclusion also would apply a fortiori. Waiting until the later school years to try to identify those in serious danger of earning poverty level incomes is surely easier than attempting this guess when the child is very young.

3. The very last point made in regard to increased per pupil expenditures deserves reiteration. That is, rates of payoff appear to be higher from adding expenditures in those school districts that are now spending relatively little. As with the first two conclusions, a weighted benefit-cost estimate would reinforce this result. The children in the lowest cost school districts have accumulated the least knowledge, and it can be inferred that they will experience the highest rates of adult poverty if educational improvements are not made.

A secondary, but also important, task of Chapters 3, 4, and 5 was to observe whether payoff rates were high enough to justify a heavy education emphasis in the war on poverty. The answer to this question depends on many issues neglected in these chapters. And even for the narrow type of measurement employed, the only relevant and defensible statement possible is an impressionistic one: with the exception of job retraining, the ratio of financial benefits to costs for educational improvements is found to be generally less than unity. Those ratios, it should be noted, did not include graduated weights according to relevant income ranges. And, as suggested by the analysis of Chapter 2, unweighted benefit-cost ratios would have to be something in excess of unity before education could be regarded as clearly superior to transfers or other forms of direct help. The case for education as an antipoverty device—

measuring poverty solely as a shortage of income—is thus not as secure as it first seemed to be.

This is hardly the end of the story. Much work remains to be done in improving the sorts of estimates attempted here and in gaining more observations. Issues not dealt with in these chapters must also be considered. We now turn our attention to this latter concern in an attempt to provide an overall reconsideration of the case for education in antipoverty efforts.

CHAPTER VI

Education's Role
in a War on Poverty

Two related tasks have been reserved for this last chapter: to examine some issues concerning education and poverty that were neglected in the preceding formal analysis, and to synthesize these new issues with the results of the formal analysis in an attempt to arrive at a balanced judgment about the role of education in a war on poverty.

In the course of deriving justifiable criteria for choosing antipoverty weapons and in attempting to estimate the private financial gain from several types of educational change, numerous issues and arguments have, for various reasons, been neglected. Sometimes it was to avoid over-complexity. Sometimes it was because no quantitative evidence could be applied satisfactorily. This chapter tries to evaluate the importance and direction of thrust of these neglected arguments and suggests what might be done in the way of approximate quantification.

Most of the arguments are ostensibly in favor of educational investment. Heightening the interest of discussing these proeducation arguments are the generally low benefit-cost ratios calculated in Chapters 3, 4, and 5. We emphasized that the empirical results presented there were primarily designed to illustrate a technique of analysis relevant to the policy issues considered and not because of high confidence in the specific policy inferences to be drawn from the benefit-cost analysis, given weaknesses and gaps in the data available. Nonetheless, the results raise serious questions about the payoff from investment in education as an antipoverty weapon. It is therefore particularly germane to examine these supplementary points.

If the preceding empirical analysis had clearly favored education as a weapon against poverty, these supplementary points would only have strengthened our conclusion. As it turns out, we are faced with the possibility that careful consideration of these neglected issues might raise the low benefit-cost ratios above 1.0. It thus seems imperative to explore the significance of these issues before venturing any "final" judgments.

The first two issues to be analyzed—intergenerational effects and supramarginal changes—are phenomena that seem to increase the antipoverty potential of education as compared to other types of policy action. The remaining issues—nonpecuniary returns, dependency, equality of opportunity, externalities, and economic growth—are matters distinguishable from the poverty reduction goal though they do have some interesting interactions with this goal.

Intergenerational Effects

It is frequently argued that improving the education of the present generation of poor people will have large positive effects on future generations as educational values pass from parent to child. From this it is sometimes speculated that educational expenditures have the unique characteristic of solving the poverty problem once and for all: a successful educational experience for one generation means that future progeny will take naturally to education and very few will end up with skills so meager as to earn only poverty level incomes. It seems clear, however, that such hopes for future generations depend upon a substantial educational gain by the current generation of the poor. Unfortunately, this first step, the large initial thrust upward, is not necessarily easy to induce. According to the computations of the preceding chapters, most special educational efforts—of the kind and scope examined—in behalf of the poor can be expected to yield only modest gains. The available evidence thus does not allow a confident and cheerful prediction that a dose of extra educational effort will immunize all future generations against poverty.

Still, small as well as large gains in learning and income are likely to be transmitted, and to that extent the poverty problems of future generations will be less serious as a result of present education efforts. Quantifying this future-generation gain and adding it to the gain of the initially educated generation would, therefore, seem to be an important refinement in our estimate of benefits. The following calculation attempts to gauge the relative importance of the intergenerational effect of education.

In estimating intergenerational benefits, it would be convenient to relate the education of the parents directly to the economic success of offspring. Unfortunately, available data do not permit such one-step procedures. The only reasonable alternative is to relate parents' educational attainment with children's, and then infer income gain from the latter.

A recent study of American families by the University of Michigan's Survey Research Center is the best source for making this intergenerational education link.[1] Information is in the form of years of education completed. Specifically, it indicates how much longer a child is likely to stay in school in the event that the family head experiences more years of education. For reasons discussed in Chapter 3 the educational advance from high school dropout to high school graduate seems to be of greatest relevance. For educational gains in this range, the Michigan study suggests that family heads who graduate (rather than drop out) raise children who end up going to school 1.1 years longer on the average.[2] In other words, two years of extra education in the first generation seem to result in more than one year of extra schooling in the next generation.

One shortcoming of this estimate is that it fails to reckon adequately with the educational attainment of the family head's wife.

[1] James N. Morgan and others, *Income and Welfare in the United States* (McGraw-Hill, 1962).

[2] *Ibid.*, p. 273.

In the large majority of cases, the family head is a married male whose wife presumably has had at least as much contact with the children as he has. Since males with relatively more education are usually married to relatively better educated wives, the apparent second-generation effect of the family head's education is in part a result of the wife's higher educational attainment. The Michigan study indicates that this is generally the case, but because the statistical analysis treats mother's and father's educations asymmetrically, it is not possible to tell if her role is more or less important than the father's.[3] In the absence of this information the fairest assumption would seem to be that both father's and mother's educations must be increased by 2 years in order for the full 1.1 years to be gained by the next generation.

Settling on this assumption is, however, only a small part of the problem. If we are to arrive at even a rough estimate of the pecuniary implications of second generation effects, several more assumptions and several numerical manipulations are required. For purposes of this illustrative calculation, the assumptions are simplistic and approximate. They consist of the following:

[3] On wife's educational attainment, the Michigan study controls only for the *difference* in attainment between husband and wife (*ibid.*, p. 274). If their attainments are the same, no further adjustment is made. Thus, if both have high school educations, they are compared directly with couples both with less than high school educations. Similarly, a high school graduate husband whose wife dropped out of high school is compared with a high school dropout husband with a grade school educated wife (etc.). If, then, the absolute level of wife's education is important to the educational attainment of children, it is clear that controlling for only husband-wife differences gives too much credit to the husband's attainment. A later calculation in the Michigan study seems to show that wife's attainment has a substantial independent influence on offspring; but it does not allow a judgment as to whose education is more influential.

It should also be noted that the relationship of 2 years of educational attainment in the first generation to 1.1 years in the second was derived after controlling for twelve factors besides attainment differences (*ibid.*, pp. 272-74). Among the most important were occupation of the family head and his highest income. Interestingly enough, the observed intergenerational transmission of education was *increased* at some attainment levels after adjustment; for instance, at the dropout to high school graduation level the unadjusted figures show only a 0.8 year gain for the second generation associated with high school graduation on the part of the first generation. An explanation for this is not readily available. In any event, the 2 year to 1.1 year relationship was meant (at least in theory) to be a gauge of the influence of parents' educational attainment independent of "all other" factors.

1. Each person in the first generation marries, and each family has (on the average) 2.5 children who are born when the married couple is 25 years of age.[4]

2. The educational improvements experienced by both the first and second generations affect males and females to the same degree. That is to say, the initial educational improvement leads to a 2 year gain by each male and female experiencing the improvement, and a 1.1 year gain by both sexes in the next generation. Males and females are also assumed to be of equal number in both generations.

3. For the second generation, the income gain associated with a given yearly gain in education is represented by cross-section earnings-by-education data from the 1960 census. As with our earlier computations, the figures are mean lifetime earnings differences between dropouts and graduates weighted by race.[5]

4. The only education gain experienced by the second generation is in the form of longer schooling (of 1.1 years); therefore, added costs of this extra schooling must be deducted from gains. As with the measure of returns, second generation costs are based on 1959 figures. These are estimated at $580 per year for income foregone[6] and $515 per year for the direct costs of high school education.[7]

---

[4] The estimate of 2.5 children per family is based on 1960 census data: for all families with own children of any age, 2.3 children is the average; for all nonwhite families, 2.9 (U.S. Department of Commerce, Bureau of the Census, *U.S. Census of Population: 1960*, "Families," PC[2]-4A, Table 4). The assumption that all children are born when parents are exactly 25 years of age is borrowed from Burton A. Weisbrod and William J. Swift, "On the Monetary Value of Education's Intergeneration Effects," *Journal of Political Economy*, Vol. 73, No. 6 (December 1965), pp. 643-49. Although they deal with the same problem we are in the midst of, there are substantial differences in approach. Most important is their use of the "option value" formula to derive an internal rate of return figure for the second generation. Skepticism about the use of this formula was noted earlier. For a critical discussion of the option value procedures see App. C.

[5] See notes in Table 5.

[6] See notes in Table 4.

[7] Direct costs are estimated by building on the current cost figure of $341 per high school pupil for urban districts (from U.S. Department of Health, Education, and Welfare, Office of Education, *Current Expenditures Per Pupil in Public School Systems: Urban School Systems, 1957-58* [1959], Table 6c). It is adjusted upward for: (1) noninstructional overhead prorated to the high school level (an 18 percent adjustment based on the ratio of operation, maintenance, and student service overheads to instruc-

To proceed from here, it is helpful to restate two of the assumptions in terms of individuals. Since every couple receiving better education results in 2.5 better educated children, each individual implies 1.25 better educated children. With this restatement, financial benefits for the second generation can be related to 2 years extra education for a "typical" member of the first generation. This will amount to the financial implication of 1.1 years education for 1.25 individuals.

Combining all the above assumptions and discounting (by 5 percent) all returns and costs back to the time when the first generation receives its improved education results in the dollar balances in the middle column of Table 11. Two different starting points were used for the discounting, one assuming that the first generation's gain of 2 years begins in nursery school (age 4), and the other that it begins at age 15. The resulting amounts seem respectably large, but it must be remembered that the assumed initial gain by the first generation was also substantial. The present value of the added income experienced by the first generation, as a result of 2 years added education, appears in the last column of Table 11. The first generation's gains far outweigh the second generation's, the latter being approximately 14 percent of the former for both starting points of the discounting process.

To reinterpret these findings in light of the analysis in earlier

---

tional costs for the entire school system [*ibid.*, Table 3]), yielding a cost of $402; (2) implicit interest and depreciation (22 percent of current costs, according to the Rude-Schultz estimate in Theodore Schultz, "Education and Economic Growth," in Nelson B. Henry (ed.), *Social Forces Influencing American Education* [University of Chicago Press, 1961], p. 85), raising cost to $490; and (3) yearly increases in per student expenditures for all levels during the late 1950's (a 5 percent adjustment to put the figures on a 1959 basis; see U.S. Department of Commerce, Bureau of the Census, *Statistical Abstract of the United States, 1962*, p. 121), resulting in the $515 cost. That figure is lower than Schultz's estimate—$568—of high school costs in 1956 ("Education and Economic Growth," pp. 65, 85) as well as his figure adjusted to a 1959 base of well over $600. Schultz adds in "additional expenses" to the student (books, supplies, extra clothes, and travel) which he assumes to be 5 percent of income foregone, but provides no evidence that these costs are any greater for a student than for a typical worker. Moreover, he derives instructional costs for high school indirectly by splitting costs for all levels of public schooling according to a 1938 study of salaries and pupil-teacher ratios that indicates costs in secondary schools are nearly twice as high as in elementary schools. Recent data (see note 10, p. 94) suggest that secondary school costs are less than 50 percent higher than elementary.

chapters, it must first be recalled that the short-run educational gains observed were typically in the form of yearly equivalent gains in achievement rather than lengthened educational careers. In Chapters 3, 4, and 5 the income effect of these yearly equivalent gains was treated as if they constituted actual continuance of schooling. If we wish to "generalize" intergenerational effects, a parallel and no less plausible assumption can be employed: that gains in yearly equivalent academic achievement experienced by the first generation have the same impact on the second generation as do longer educational careers experienced by the first genera-

TABLE 11

First and Second Generation Income Benefits from
First Generation's Improved Education

Improved Education Begins	Second Generation Income[a]	First Generation Income[b]
Age 15	$909	$6,349
Age 4	$531	$3,798

[a] Net of extra costs for a 2 year education gain by first generation.
[b] For 2 year education gain.

tion. Thus, we might say that a two year gain in academic achievement on the part of the first generation—even though no elongation of schooling is involved—yields the same benefits for the second generation as that calculated in Table 11. And, to generalize still further, it can be argued that income gains computed in the earlier chapters on a one generation basis should all be adjusted upward by 14 percent in order to take account of the financial gains to the next generation. This new revised figure could then be compared to initial costs to yield a benefit-cost estimate adjusted for second generation effects.

It goes without saying that the above calculation is extremely tenuous. It depends upon many of the assumptions used in Chapters 3, 4, and 5, plus a few more. The nub of the problem is attempting to predict, on the basis of current relationships, what will happen a good many years from now. This difficulty is present in all the earlier calculations, and it is unavoidably compounded in the estimation of second generation benefits. And, as in many of the earlier calculations, there is no sure way to establish whether the estimate based on current relationships is overoptimistic or overpessimistic.[8]

In addition to the technical problems of estimation, it is no less important to keep in mind that transfers or other forms of direct help may also have favorable repercussions on academic and economic careers of children in the families directly benefited. Several observers have argued this position forcefully, and the only systematic research available supports this view.[9] To put the matter another way, it is probably possible to "break the cycle of poverty" at many points. An important implication of this is that the calculated second generation benefits attributed to education may not constitute a clear net advantage as compared to direct help. If education does have a net advantage along these lines, it likely is not as great as our calculations suggest.

[8] On the cost side, the assumptions have been more charitable than those used by other researchers (see note 41, p. 59 and note 7, p. 104). The great uncertainty, though, is with the nature of earnings differentials connected with education several decades from now. Our earlier discussion suggested that an "ability" adjustment should more than cancel out the growth in differentials (pp. 57-59). But for decades hence, this is a much more dubious proposition.

[9] S. Michael Miller and Martin Rein make the point in the following fashion: "Would increasing the income of a poor family do as much to increase the children's interest in further advance as would specific training programs? We are not confident that the results of a study of these alternative ways of spending poverty funds would support a training program, separate from improving the economic conditions of families and neighborhoods. True, *some* youth would escape from poverty more easily than before, but would the greater number of youth? Economic and social change may have to precede the call for individual responsibility and adjustment." ("The War on Poverty: Perspectives and Prospects," in Ben B. Seligman [ed.], *Poverty as a Public Issue* [Free Press, 1965], p. 289.) Harry G. Johnson notes the "strong possibility that the preoccupation of parents with the earning of money—especially in broken homes—is an important factor in the perpetuation of poverty among the children of the poor" (in "The Economics of Poverty," *American Economic Review*, Vol. 55, No. 2 [May 1965], pp. 543-44). The best and most relevant empirical work available appears to be Robert A. Dentler and Mary Ellen Warshauer, *Big City Dropouts* (New York: Center for Urban Education, 1965). Based on a multiple correlation (cross-section) analysis of 131 large cities, this study concludes that a fair amount of the variance among cities in dropout rates and in adult functional illiteracy is statistically explained by rates of Aid to Families with Dependent Children payments, and by spending rates on (noneducational) public projects such as hospitals and parks (*ibid.*, pp. 28-31, 46-54).

Supramarginal Change

One of the implicit assumptions underlying all the previous calculations is that a program of antipoverty education results in only a
"marginal" change in the educational composition of the labor
force. That is, the increased flow of better educated workers, due
to antipoverty programs, is assumed to be only a small increase
over the regular flow and a relatively insignificant addition to the
total supply of all such workers. Similarly, the reduction in supply
of all poorly educated workers is assumed to be insignificant as
compared to the total supply. Without this assumption of marginal change it is difficult to justify the use of earnings differentials
in the recent past as a basis for estimating returns from current
programs. The presumption that contemplated educational changes
do not greatly alter the composition of the work force, and that
relative earnings will therefore not be perceptibly influenced by
such changes, is a common characteristic of practically all recent
work in calculating the returns to education. And it would seem
a fair presumption in this study as well, as long as one thinks in
terms of the relatively small size of current antipoverty efforts. But
when one speaks of eliminating all poverty and plans to accomplish
this mainly through educational improvements, it becomes apparent that shifting wage relationships must be reckoned with.

Several economists have pondered the possibility of shifts in
earning relationships brought on by a large dose of increased education for the poor. Their judgment by and large has been that
such shifts reinforce the case for education. The point emphasized
is that even the poor people who do *not* receive improved education experience benefit, due to the shrinking supplies of poorly educated workers.[10] The smaller supplies mean higher earnings for

[10] This line of argument can be found in A. C. Pigou, *The Economics of Welfare*
(4th ed.; Macmillan, 1932), p. 753; Committee for Economic Development (CED),
Raising Low Incomes Through Improved Education (CED, September 1965), pp. 18-
19; Thomas N. Carver, "A Conservative's Ideas on Economic Reform," *Quarterly
Journal of Economics,* Vol. 74, No. 4 (November 1960), pp. 536-42; and James Tobin,
"On Improving the Economic Status of the Negro," *Dædalus,* Vol. 94, No. 4 (Fall
1965), pp. 888-89.

the poor and poorly educated; this, it is argued, should surely count as progress toward the goal of complete poverty elimination.

Those who have made this argument have not developed it much beyond the stage of saying that higher earnings among the neglected poor is a desirable secondary effect of antipoverty education. Despite its apparent simplicity, the contention is extremely difficult to integrate into a benefit-cost framework.

Let us suppose that the analysis, based on the assumption of a marginal change in better educated workers, yields a benefit-cost ratio less than unity. This supposition is supported by much of the illustrative analysis presented above and, in any event, seems the only circumstance worth considering in that what we really want to know is whether recognition of a "supramarginal" effect might incline us to use education when we might not otherwise. If we employ the perspective of the representative citizen as developed in Chapter 2, the problem might be simply phrased as follows: While educating a group of poorly educated individuals entails higher costs than necessary to bring about a given income improvement for the newly educated group, the remaining educationally neglected individuals will require a smaller amount of transfers per individual in order to arrive at a respectable level of income. Of course, workers who are already better educated will experience some decline in incomes, but perhaps this decline still leaves them with earnings above the poverty range. This manner of reasoning is illustrated in Figure 1.

In this diagram, the downward sloping line represents the demand curve for poorly educated workers and thus relates the supply of such workers to their earned income level. This supply is assumed to be insensitive to changes in earnings but alterable by the provision of better education to some of these workers which, in turn, allows them to compete for higher paying jobs requiring better educational backgrounds. On the horizontal axis of the diagram, let:

$X_t =$ the initial supply of poorly educated workers

$X_t - X_r =$ the number of poorly educated workers who are given a better education

$X_r =$ the number of poorly educated workers left poorly educated.

FIGURE 1. *Effect of Reduced Numbers of Poorly Educated Workers on Their Income Level*

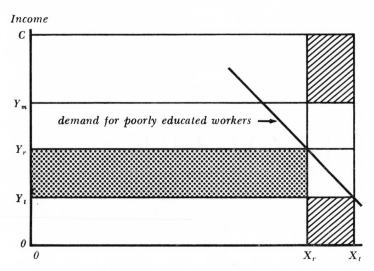

Number of poorly educated workers

On the vertical axis, let:

$Y_t =$ the initial earned income level for poorly educated workers

$Y_r =$ the earned income level for the poorly educated workers who remain poorly educated

$Y_m =$ the "bottom" poverty line as defined in Chapter 2

$C =$ the constant cost of better education for one worker that is sufficient to bring his earnings to Y_m.

To make costs and income commensurable, the latter is assumed to refer to present value of lifetime income. For the purposes of this exercise, earned income levels as well as the "bottom" poverty line are interpreted in this fashion rather than in the more customary terms of yearly amounts.

As will be recalled from Chapter 2, the "bottom" poverty line refers to the level of income to which all individuals would be increased if one-to-one transfers were the only antipoverty device available. It would follow that, in order to bring the entire group of workers earning incomes of Y_r up to the bottom poverty line, a total transfer cost of $X_t(Y_m - Y_t)$ would have to be incurred. If we instead educate $X_t - X_r$ workers at C cost per worker, costs for this subgroup are greater—as compared to the straight transfer case—by an amount equal to $(X_t - X_r)(C - Y_m + Y_t)$. This extra cost is depicted by the striped areas in Figure 1. Presuming, then, that this succeeds in raising the incomes of the $Y_t - Y_r$ workers up to only Y_m, it appears a less preferable course of action to our representative citizen than straight transfers. But, less transfers are required to raise each of the remaining X_r workers to a Y_m level. The transfer bill for this group is reduced by $Y_r - Y_t$ for each worker; and the total transfer saving, depicted by the shaded area in Figure 1, is equal to $X_r(Y_r - Y_t)$. If this area turns out to be greater than the sum of the two striped areas, as it does in Figure 1, it may be concluded that educating $X_r - X_t$ workers was a less expensive way to bring all workers up to a Y_m level.

The above analysis can thus be summarized in the expression

$$X_r(Y_r - Y_t) \gtrless (X_t - X_r)(C - Y_m + Y_t) \qquad (1)$$

where net tax saving occurs only when the left-hand side of (1) is greater than the right. To simplify, $Y_r - Y_t$ can be replaced by $(X_t - X_r) \Delta Y/\Delta X$, where $\Delta Y/\Delta X$ represents the absolute value of the slope of the demand curve for poorly educated labor. $X_t - X_r$ is now common to both sides of the inequality and can be removed without affecting the comparison, leaving us with

$$X_r \frac{\Delta Y}{\Delta X} \gtrless C - Y_m + Y_t. \qquad (2)$$

This makes clear the minimum data needs for estimating whether giving better education to a discrete number of poorly educated workers does, or does not, result in a net tax savings. In (2) it is apparent that an exact balancing of the income gain experienced by the newly educated workers with the cost of education results in a zero value for the right-hand side of this expression. At that point, net tax savings must occur as long as there are some poorly educated workers left behind and the slope of the demand curve for poorly educated workers is negative. When the cost of education exceeds the income gain by the newly educated, the result can go either way, depending on the relationships in (2).

This is surely not the only way to formalize the argument that supramarginal change might make us more favorably inclined to using education. However, it seems to be the simplest, although even this very simple version of the argument raises formidable measurement problems.

Of greatest concern is the difficulty in identifying empirically a separate demand schedule for "poorly educated" workers. Workers with different amounts of education and training hold similar jobs at similar pay. High school graduates and high school dropouts (for instance) are not noncompeting groups; and, at least at present, there seems to be no credible procedure for estimating the elasticity of substitution between these two groups. This problem, as well as several others, disallows a serious attempt at estimating the empirical importance of this argument.

A second difficulty is estimating the effect of transfer payments on work incentives. Even graduated transfers would likely deter some individuals from working or from working as much as they otherwise might. The amount of such work disincentive is difficult to predict, and so would be the net effect of this on the final transfer bill. The workers who leave the labor force would have to be paid more to achieve a given distribution goal; but the shrinkage in the supply of poorly educated workers would result in higher earned incomes for those who remain in the labor force. For this latter group, less transfer payments per individual would be required.

A third problem is assessing the change in income experienced by "better" educated workers that results from expanding their numbers. If there is no excess demand for such workers, an expansion in their numbers will have some detrimental effect on their income position, and some of this might take place in a range relevant for poverty considerations. In terms of the framework of Chapter 2, the incomes of those who recede below the "top" poverty line should have their loss weighted and added in as a "cost" (or as a reduction in benefits).

Still another consideration is the change in average costs that would likely accompany an educational push of supramarginal proportions. In particular, the supply of the right sorts of teachers is probably quite inelastic in the short run, and an attempt to change quickly the quality and magnitude of education on a nationwide scale would, to some extent, result in higher teachers' salaries (and a higher cost for education) without a commensurate increase in services.

Until the above problems are resolved, there seems little point in attempting a quantitative estimate of how much the effects of supramarginal changes might alter educational decisions. All that can be stated is the direction of influence: an educational change thought to be supramarginal might, in an antipoverty context, incline us to accept benefit-cost ratios that are less than unity.

Psychic Returns

As stated in Chapter 1, the improved education of the poor can potentially give rise to many sorts of benefits. Our attention has been fixed on the enhanced material well-being of those in poverty. Though there were good reasons for this narrow focus, there is nevertheless an obligation to suggest how the other benefits of education might be evaluated and perhaps quantified. Much has been written by economists on this valuation problem, but little in the context of an antipoverty effort. The comments in this and the following sections are aimed at the special considerations present in this context.

Probably the most frequently mentioned role of education is the development of character and intellect as ends in themselves, independent of the financial gain these may bring. Economists usually label such benefits "psychic returns" or the "consumption element" of education. Among nonmonetary benefits subsumed under this heading are the satisfaction of working in an interesting and pleasant job and the immediate pleasures of experiencing a good education. Although many have urged that psychic returns be given a monetary weight, no serious empirical research has been attempted along these lines, and few specific research sugges-tions have been submitted. There is little reason to think that such an estimate can be accomplished with any more ease in the context of poverty.

One possible way to derive a monetary value for individual psy-chic returns is to canvass the persons experiencing the education, or perhaps their parents. The student or parent might be asked: How much would you pay for a better education if you antici-pated that this education brought about *no* change in lifetime money income? A perfectly foresightful individual could conceiv-ably discount the joys and pains he expects to flow from his (or his child's) educational experience, and a reply could be phrased in terms of a single dollar-and-cents figure. While actually conduct-ing a survey along these lines is probably out of the question, it can be argued that this valuation procedure should be imagined by the people charged with making final decisions. By keeping in mind what is known about the preferences of those in poverty, one might thus avoid a paternalistic judgment about psychic returns.

On the other hand, it could be argued that reshaping the prefer-ences of the poor is an important and unavoidable element of an antipoverty education program. Instilling the "right" sort of atti-tudes about work and ambition is frequently considered a way in which better education reduces poverty. And if we are willing to bring about these taste changes, there is little reason for squeam-ishness in making the judgment that poor people should be taught to appreciate educational values more than they do or in reasoning that the poor will have a higher regard for such values after the education is experienced. But even if the decision is to be frankly paternalistic, this does not dispense with the need to determine the degree to which specific educational improvements for the poor do result in differences in outlook, style of life, etc. And on that, I have encountered no compelling evidence that indicates even the general magnitude of such changes.

If we wish eventually to say more about this question, interdis-ciplinary studies are required. Envisioning the shape of this re-search is difficult, and considerable subjectivity will probably have to be employed in interpreting the findings. Unfortunately, the only alternative to such research is introspection and the chance anecdote.

Reducing Dependency

Another appealing aspect of an education solution to poverty is avoidance of a "handout" connotation. There is little point in reviewing the plentiful and well known rhetoric on this point. It would seem useful, however, to discuss the main facets of thought behind this sentiment.

On the general theme of dependency there are at least three related variations suggesting that education is a form of action superior to transfers and most other types of direct help. The first of these was mentioned earlier: that direct redistribution, even in the form of a negative income tax, is bound to produce some disincentive to work, implying in turn that the transfer bill may be higher than initially anticipated. Though there appear to be no convincing estimates of the magnitude of work disincentive under various transfer schemes, such measurements are within the realm of possibility, and an "adjusted" cost for a transfer program might be derived that could, without great difficulty, be integrated into an evaluative framework similar to that developed in Chapter 2.[11]

Two other points cannot be assessed so directly. The first is the argument that anyone who fails to work as much or as hard as he might—because of the disincentive of transfer payments—is in essence "voluntarily" poor and thus "undeserving" of an income supplement. A related argument is that even if transfers do not discourage a maximum work effort, the recipients are nevertheless partially dependent upon the state, and this might be harmful for self-esteem or at least not as dignified as earning one's way out of poverty.[12] On the basis of these two judgments, some observers

[11] A review of available research bearing on the disincentive effect of transfers can be found in Christopher Green, *Negative Taxes and the Poverty Problem* (Brookings Institution, 1967).

[12] *Economic Report of the President, January 1964, Together with the Annual Report of the Council of Economic Advisers* states that "Americans want to *earn* the

seem to feel that education is a preferable antipoverty instrument even if it requires exceedingly high costs to achieve the same antipoverty goal. Nevertheless, it is likely that most people "have their price" on this issue, and at some very low payoff rate for education, there are few who would continue to insist on an education approach.

This does not mean an easy consensus is attainable. Many will continue to view all transfers as odious devices of last resort, and others will consider transfers a relatively harmless extension of progressive taxation. On balance, the public image of direct redistribution seems to be unfavorable. Attitudes toward public employment and subsidized housing are not much better. Education, in comparison, is relatively free of the handout stigma. Thus, for this reason alone, a financial benefit-cost ratio for education of less than unity might be tolerated for antipoverty purposes.

It must be remembered, however, that a set of programs designed to eliminate poverty *must* include at least some transfer elements. Some poverty afflicted members of the community are beyond working age or incapacitated in various ways. For these, education may do no material good at all. And this raises the question of what to do for those whom education can help only a very little. The gradation of the benefits from education, from those cases where little is gained up to those who can be helped a great deal, needs to be specified; and the sentiment in favor of education must be given quantitative content in order to specify when education or a transfer type program is more appropriate. Reaching a public consensus on this issue that has quantitative content is of course very difficult, but there is no reason to think it is any more difficult than the decision on where to establish poverty lines.

American standard of living by their own efforts and contributions. It will be far better, even if more difficult, to equip and to permit the poor of the Nation to produce and to earn the additional $11 billion, and more" (p. 77). A similar view is expressed by the Committee for Economic Development: ". . . as among ways of helping the least fortunate it is surely better, in most cases, to help them to improve their earning capacity than simply to transfer income to them from others—better in terms of the burden on others as well as in terms of the dignity of those assisted" (*Raising Low Incomes Through Improved Education*, p. 21).

Equality of Opportunity

Much of what was said in the two preceding sections applies to the goal of equal opportunity. Once more the issue boils down to making a subjective judgment about the importance of the goal and deciding upon the degree to which this inclines us to use an education approach to poverty.

It is especially important, however, to remember that equality in expenditures per pupil is no guarantee that academic outcomes will be the same for children of low and high socioeconomic status. Indeed, evidence from the Project Talent survey indicates that the achievement levels of low status pupils in the *highest* expenditure school districts are still much lower than those of high status pupils in the *lowest* expenditure districts.[13] This raises the question of how equality of opportunity is to be defined. Should the definition be in terms of the quality and magnitude of the resources devoted to the education of low and high status pupils, or should it be in terms

---

[13] The table below contrasts test score performance for pupils in the bottom socioeconomic quintile with that of pupils in the next-to-highest quintile. The figures refer to the North and West subsample of Project Talent; all pupils took the tests near the end of twelfth grade; and test scores are averages of the academic and nonacademic test composites. All definitions are the same as those in Table 7.

School District Expenditures per Pupil	Mean Test Score for Low Status Pupils, in Yearly Equivalents	Mean Test Score for High Status Pupils, in Yearly Equivalents
Less than $200	9.82	11.92
$200-$300	10.25	12.82
$300-$400	10.32	13.17
$400-$500	10.53	13.06
More than $500	10.43	13.88

Scores above 12.0 should *not* be interpreted as equivalent to the performance of college freshmen; they are simple linear extrapolations based on the difference in mean test scores between high school grade levels. (Information from Project Talent Data Bank.)

of academic accomplishment and (or) the degree of actual social and economic mobility? Expenditures per pupil and achievement test scores are only proxies for these two standards, but they make clear that the difference between the two standards is very great.[14]

There is no question that equal attainment is a much more ambitious goal than equal educational quality (or quantity). It may even be—given the fact that formal education is only part of the total learning experience and is not the sole contributor to the child's growth and development—that, under existing arrangements, the goal is unattainable. Since socioeconomic background still makes a great difference in the degree to which individuals can profit from education, formal equality in educational expenditures is a milestone of dubious significance.

The immediate reason for raising this definitional matter is to emphasize that meaningful equality of opportunity is not around a nearby corner easily reached by an education approach to poverty. The choice of weapons in the war on poverty, at least on the present scale, can only make a small contribution toward complete realization of the equality of opportunity goal as stated in its more ambitious and probably more meaningful form. The contribution should not, of course, be ignored. But it is worth noting once more that direct help to poor families should have some positive effect on the academic performance of children, and thus also make a contribution to the goal of equal opportunity. In summary, the goal of equal opportunity can be viewed as a valid, though hardly an overriding, reason why we might be inclined to emphasize education in an antipoverty campaign.

[14] Most recent commentary argues that social justice does demand something more than equal amounts of resources (of apparently equal quality) devoted to the public schools attended by the poor and by the affluent. Indeed, it is very difficult to find a contemporary essay that argues that equality in resources has any special interest at all. There is also general skepticism that equal educational services can even be defined. The typical teacher, having "middle class" predilections, is frequently thought to be so hostile and out of touch with lower class children that he (she) in essence becomes a very different sort of person when confronting a classroom of slum children as compared to a classroom of children from the suburbs. (See Kenneth Clark, *Dark Ghetto* [Harper & Row, 1965], Chap. 5.)

Externalities

As in the case of psychic returns, many diverse elements are summed up by the term "externalities." As argued in Chapter 2, the removal of poverty can itself be described and analyzed as an externality. This analysis depended upon empathic concern for those with low incomes. The more typical case of an external benefit involves more selfish motivation; and many of these external benefits may justifiably affect our choice of antipoverty weapons.

Other studies have devoted ample discussion to the numerous externalities that might flow from improved education.[15] Possible externalities range from the social benefit of having a better informed electorate to the chance that an extra dose of education will spark a latent genius into becoming a great benefactor of mankind. While many of these are very speculative and assessable only in a highly subjective way, some categories of external benefits are at least partially amenable to direct dollar measurement. Of special interest here are various forms of antisocial behavior—for example, juvenile delinquency—whose suppression requires large public expenditures. Improved education for underprivileged youths could very likely lower the frequency of such behavior and thus the costs of policing, incarceration, and treatment. Cost savings can be used as an approximation of the magnitude of benefit.

While cost savings of this nature are often mentioned, information on the determinants of antisocial behavior has not been sufficiently complete to encourage a quantitative estimate of what this element might add to the benefits of improved education. However, a recent study by Fleisher on the determinants of juvenile delinquency permits a rough calculation of possible cost savings.[16]

[15] See especially Burton A. Weisbrod, *External Benefits of Public Education: An Economic Analysis* (Princeton University, Department of Economics, Industrial Relations Section, 1964); Weisbrod, "Education and Investment in Human Capital," *Journal of Political Economy*, Vol. 70, No. 5, Supplement (October 1962), pp. 106-23.

[16] Belton M. Fleisher, "The Effect of Income on Delinquency," *American Economic Review*, Vol. 56, No. 1 (March 1966), pp. 118-37.

Fleisher does not study directly the association between education and delinquency, but he manages to calculate a convincing estimate of the relation between family income and delinquency. This he does by a cross-section multiple regression analysis of lower income groups in 101 large cities. He concludes that "in extremely delinquent areas, . . . a 10 percent rise in income may be expected to reduce delinquency rates by between 15 and 20 percent when the income change occurs in highly delinquent areas and is of the type that will reduce the number of broken families as well." In Fleisher's words, "it appears that the effect of income on delinquency is not a small one."[17] But here we must be cautious. "Not small" is a relative thing. And for our purposes, it is necessary to put Fleisher's results in terms of absolute dollar amounts before we can hope to get a clear picture of how it compares to the sorts of magnitudes we have calculated so far.

First, it can be estimated that a 10 percent income gain means about a $300 increase in yearly family income for those residing in "high delinquency areas."[18] Number of arrests per year per 1,000 males younger than 25 is Fleisher's unit of account on the delinquency side of the equation. A 15 to 20 percent drop on this index amounts to roughly five fewer arrests per 1,000 young males.[19] Now it might be asked, what is the *total* income gain for a given community required to reduce arrests by five? For purposes of a rough estimate, it seems fair to assume (a) that families have an average size of four individuals, and (b) that one out of every four

---

[17] *Ibid.*, pp. 134-35.

[18] This presumes that the income gain occurs among low income groups only. Fleisher worked with mean family incomes in the second and fourth quartiles of income. Technical problems prevented him from dealing with the lowest income quartile, but he argues that the relationship between second quartile incomes and delinquency is a good proxy for the effect of gains in the lowest quartile (*ibid.*, pp. 132, 134). A 10 percent gain in income in the second quartile amounts to about $470 gain in family income for high delinquency areas (*ibid.*, p. 126). For the present calculation it is assumed that a $300 income gain among the very lowest income groups has the same delinquency prevention effect as does a $470 gain for slightly better off families.

[19] *Ibid.*, pp. 134-35. "High delinquency" areas have an arrest rate of 24 per 1,000. The figure of 5 fewer arrests entails the assumption that no income gains occur in the upper ranges of income simultaneously with the gains in the lower ranges. If gains did occur simultaneously in the upper ranges, the calculated reduction in arrests (according to Fleisher's estimates) would not be as great (*ibid.*, pp. 132-34).

individuals is a male under 25 years of age. With these assumptions, it follows that 1,000 families are necessary in order to have 1,000 young males present. Thus, if each family gains $300, the total income gain required to have five fewer arrests amounts to $300,000.

As a final step we might estimate how much a community saves in police costs when a reduction in delinquency results in five fewer arrests per year. In 1960 (the base year in our earlier calculations and in Fleisher's) arrests in cities totaled approximately 5 million, and police costs about $1.3 billion.[20] Dividing the latter figure by the former suggests that arrests cost $260 apiece. That is to say, if five fewer arrests are needed, and police costs decline proportionately, a savings of $1,300 can be anticipated. And even this is a liberal estimate since the marginal costs are undoubtedly below the average.

Thus, a total income gain of $300,000 in high delinquency areas can be said to bring about a $1,300 reduction in the needed costs of public safety. This cost reduction amounts to less than 0.5 percent of the direct income gain. Of course, there can—and should— be added to this cost reduction a variety of other savings and benefits: for example, the costs of the judicial process, of damage caused by delinquency, of the "life of crime" that the first delinquency may lead to, etc. It is, however, hard to imagine that these would substantially alter the order of magnitude of the result.

If it is assumed that education results in a reduced inclination toward crime solely through the effect of higher earned incomes, then the above estimates would seem directly applicable. But if improved education, in and of itself, results in a higher degree of socialization and restraint in its recipient, then the above figure would be an underestimate. This is because education and income are not perfectly correlated. Hence, two communities that differ by exactly $300 in family income will not generally have average

<hr />

[20] The figure on arrests is calculated from data in U.S. Department of Commerce, Bureau of the Census, *Statistical Abstract of the United States, 1962*, p. 153. The published figure applies to cities that include 73 percent of all individuals living in cities. This total was multiplied by 1.4 to estimate arrests in all cities and thus make the arrest figure comparable with the police expenditure information. The latter was taken from U.S. Department of Commerce, *Compendium of City Government Finances in 1960*, C-CF60-No. 2 (1961), Table I, p. 8.

educational attainments such that we would have predicted this $300 difference. Rather, the differential educational attainments will be somewhat smaller. Therefore, it might be reasoned that if the increase in a community's educational level is sufficient to raise the average family income by $300, the reduction in juvenile delinquency would be greater than is indicated by the straight cross-section comparison of "lower-income" groups with different levels of income.

To derive a more accurate estimate we need to separate the effects of increases in earned income, income transfers, and educational attainments. Fleisher was not able to do so, and his summary of related research indicates that no one else has been able to.[21] But despite the obvious shortcomings of the above calculation and the numbers on which it is based, the order of magnitude is nevertheless intriguing. Moreover, it is doubtful whether a more careful analysis would greatly change the general conclusion that savings in the public safety costs of juvenile delinquency are a very small fraction of the direct income gains experienced because of education. In addition, it must be remembered that other forms of antipoverty action, including direct transfers, should also be expected to have positive effects on the rate of antisocial acts.

Thus, at least for the time being, it is difficult to argue that consideration of the tangible savings in social costs should very much alter the direction or magnitude of our antipoverty efforts.

Economic Growth

Much of the scholarly interest in the economics of education, especially in the early 1960's, stemmed from the belief that increased education would contribute to accelerated economic growth. Of late, the goal of growth has faded somewhat from the spotlight in domestic policy debates. Nevertheless, a few brief comments seem called for on how this goal relates to the preceding analysis.

One of the reasons for thinking that increased education might encourage growth is the earlier observation that the American

[21] "The Effect of Income on Delinquency," pp. 133-34 (footnote).

economy has experienced historical growth in national income far in excess of what would be anticipated on the basis of historical increases in men and machines. A substantial part of this unexplained gap may be due to various externalities in production generated by an increasingly better educated labor force. Exactly how much can be attributed to increased education, and how much to other economic developments, is still very much an open question. It is, therefore, not clear whether the growth-inducing externalities of education justify special emphasis on expanding this particular sector of the economy as opposed to other sectors. Moreover, it is worth noting that technological breakthroughs are what most economists seem to have in mind when they cite growth externalities as a by-product of education. This suggests that the very advanced levels of education are chiefly responsible for this variety of externality. When talking about the provision of respectable elementary and secondary education for underprivileged children, this consideration might justifiably be neglected.

Another and more palpable way in which antipoverty education might contribute to the goal of growth is the earnings gains directly experienced by the poor. If increases in money national income per se are considered socially laudable, it could be argued that the increased earnings of the poor should, in some fashion, be "double counted"—once for their contribution to poverty reduction and again for their contribution to economic growth.

It should not be forgotten, however, that there are other ways of stimulating economic growth. Tax incentives to corporate investment is one of these ways. The before-tax rate of return to corporate capital has been estimated to be about 12 percent[22]—well above the implied rate of return for the changes in general education considered in Chapters 3, 4, and 5. This implies that increasing corporate incentives would yield considerably more growth per dollar of present consumption sacrificed than would antipoverty education—at least of the kind and size examined. If growth is what we are after, the education of the poor would be only one of many ways—and not necessarily one of the better ways—to that end.

Still, the use of education now rather than of transfers in the fu-

[22] Gary S. Becker, *Human Capital* (National Bureau of Economic Research, 1964), p. 120.

ture does imply that total savings and investment are increased. This in turn should reduce the felt need to stimulate investment in physical capital. It might be argued that investment in education would permit a reduction, say, of the investment tax credit since part of the growth goal is being achieved via education. The consequent amount of revenue savings could then be added to the benefits perceived by the typical citizen. A calculation of this sort is not as simple as it might first appear. Clear specification of growth targets is required. The effectiveness of tax incentives in increasing investment must also be known. And one must take into account the fact that less stimulus to physical investment will likely have some detrimental effect on the future incomes of the presently poor.

Summary of Additional Benefits

The analysis of this chapter does not add a great deal to the "case for education" as it applies to the goal of poverty reduction. Intergenerational benefits turn out to be a small fraction of first generation benefits. And the implication of supramarginal change can, at present, be expressed in only a qualitative fashion: the extension of education may be justified somewhat beyond the point where simple benefit-cost ratios have a value of unity.

The other anticipated advantages of education are another matter. If one feels strongly enough about the psychic benefits of education, the corrupting influence of transfer payments, the goal of equal opportunity, or the need for economic growth, education might be a preferred course of action even if its measurable contribution to poverty reduction is small per dollar of cost. For most of these goals, additional measurements can be of assistance, but they cannot dictate what the trade off should be between reducing poverty and furthering other social aims.

An earlier caution deserves repeating: alternatives to education may do nearly as much (and in some cases, more) to achieve some of the "side" benefits frequently anticipated from education. It is not enough to say that improved education has a second generation effect, promotes more equal opportunity, and reduces antisocial behavior. Simple income transfers should, to some extent, do the same. And more specific forms of direct help (for example, improved housing) may give rise to secondary effects every bit as great as those accruing from an equal dollar amount of improved education. Future measurements and policy judgments should not ignore this possibility.

Finally, it should be noted that the considerations raised in this chapter could also alter our preferences for different types of educational change. In particular, vocational education may not be clearly preferable to general education as was suggested by the benefit-cost calculations. General education probably results in bigger second generation effects, greater psychic returns, and more externalities than does vocational education.

Warnings to the Policy Maker

Is it possible to arrive at any clear-cut policy conclusions out of this study? In particular, what does the analysis imply for the role of education in an antipoverty effort? Before trying to answer this question, let us address ourselves briefly to the question of whether the low rates of financial return calculated in this study make any sense. It should be emphasized once more that these calculations relied upon very unsure assumptions. Still, they seem to be the most reasonable assumptions available, and they are generally consistent with what other students of the economics of education have judged to be appropriate. But is the outcome reasonable? Can it really be that improved general education results in average financial gains that are less than costs, therefore implying a fortiori that education is a relatively expensive and inefficient means of bringing people out of poverty?

One possible explanation for our empirical results is that the "culture of poverty" militates strongly against educational progress for the children of this culture. On the other hand, it is yet to be established with any certainty that educational improvements affecting more affluent individuals give rise to payoff rates that are significantly better than the ones calculated for individuals in poverty. From the available evidence, it is not clear that relatively high status students profit a great deal more from improvements in educational quality.[23]

An alternative and more convincing explanation stems from the earlier discussion in this chapter of education's numerous potential by-products. Many of these by-products have a social and non-pecuniary nature. And if social decisions have, in the past, been influenced by the hope of receiving these by-products, it could be argued that education already has been expanded and intensified to the point where it can no longer be justified in terms of direct financial profitability. If greater equality of opportunity, improvement in citizenship, and the perpetuation of a cultural heritage were considerations entering into past educational decisions (can this be doubted?), it is not surprising that a still greater intensification of our educational efforts may result in private financial gains that fall short of costs.

Thus, it is possible to provide a very traditional economic rationale for the low rates of return on improved education. Economists have long recognized that differential rates of return, for similar factors of production, can often be explained on the basis of compensating nonfinancial advantages. And, to the degree that society perceives large nonpecuniary advantages in education and has reacted rationally to this perception, a similar explanation is available for the low rate of financial payoff for the programs examined in this study. These low rates of return do not belie the existence of capital market imperfections. One can simply conclude that these are more than counterbalanced by the influence of governmental support of education.

What then should be said about the high rates of return (discussed in Chapter 1) associated with undertaking additional levels

[23] As mentioned earlier, the calculations performed with low status pupils in the Project Talent sample (Chap. 4) were duplicated for pupils in the next-to-highest socioeconomic quintile. Though the spread of scores between the lowest and the highest expenditure categories was greater than the spread among low status pupils, the weighted-average (yearly equivalent) gain in test scores associated with a $100 increase in expenditures was practically the same for both groups. See Table 9 and the related discussion in the text.

of schooling? These payoff rates suggest that an individual who chooses (voluntarily) to undertake continued study, at any educational level, tends to earn a high rate of return on his own investment and a high before-tax rate of return on total resource costs. The answer to this apparent contradiction with the findings of the present study is that inducing heavier flows of students through additional increments of education may require an expensive program of counseling and persuasion. It follows, then, that these previously calculated rates of high return for voluntary school continuance are not necessarily inconsistent with the conclusion that available policy alternatives yield low payoff rates. The students involved—and their motivation—are, after all, quite different.

Thus, while it cannot be stated with certainty that improved education (of the kind and scope examined) results in income gains to the poor that are less than costs, it is useful to discuss policy implications that might follow under the assumption that a heavy emphasis on general education is not the most efficient way to approach poverty alleviation. Even this presumption does not lead to hard and fast rules about the direction of policy. Any one of several alternative policy attitudes can be adopted. Depending on temperament and value premises, a policy maker might reasonably choose any one of the following positions.

First, a policy maker could feel that the alleviation of poverty is only one of many benefits. The intangible benefits of education (social and private) may be considered much more important than the goal of generating income gains. Thus, a heavy emphasis on the improved education of the poor could be justified even if only a relatively small amount of poverty is alleviated as a result.

Second, he may feel that large amounts of transfers and other direct help are simply out of the question. The handout connotation of such approaches may result in a near-absolute constraint. Therefore, even though the alleviation of poverty is paramount in the mind of a policy maker, he may feel compelled to choose an apparently less efficient approach to this goal.

Third, he may feel that poverty is more than a matter of income and that while income is changed by transfers, the changes he seeks—in attitude, motivation, etc.—are only the result of education and other nontransfer programs.

Fourth, it might be argued that the evidence of low payoff rates to relatively modest educational improvements suggests that revolutionary changes in the school system are called for. It might be argued that slum schools should be saturated with vast amounts of new personnel and equipment, thus bringing matters to a new threshold where low status students would end up gaining economic competence worth much more than the costs of the saturation. However, the cross-section analysis with Project Talent schools, which dealt with reasonably large dollar differences in expenditures per student, did not establish that large changes are any more efficient than small ones. It may be that the real need lies in a revolution of attitudes, organization, and approach of public school systems. While it is unclear where one turns for evidence on the efficacy or permanence of such a revolution, it is not unreasonable for the policy maker to prefer the gamble in this direction. Additionally, he may feel that social attitudes have changed and with them the returns to increased expenditure and effort.

Fifth, the evidence of low payoff rates might be used to justify a major reorientation of the war on poverty, in the direction of a heavier emphasis on transfers and other forms of direct help. A strong devotion to the goal of poverty alleviation, an absence of serious constraints on policy choice, and a distrust of revolutions could prompt such a reorientation.

Finally, one could argue that education and direct help expenditures should be designed to work in close tandem. A somewhat heavier emphasis, than now exists, on direct help programs could be justified, but with the proviso that they be tied closely to education programs. If there is a (formal or informal) budget constraint, of some sort, this implies that less of the new spending on antipoverty programs should be channeled into education. This, however, might result in little, if any, loss in terms of foregone improvements in educational performance. Indeed, additional marginal expenditures aimed directly at improving the economic well-being of poor families may do more for educational performance than marginal expenditures in the schools. Chapters 3, 4, and 5 provide many clues that socioeconomic class is a powerful determinant of educational outcomes; and a relatively small improvement along this dimension, as a result of government programs, may lead to substantial improvements along the dimension of educational performance.

This possibility makes doubly difficult the search for an optimum mix between education and direct help. But to ignore possible complementarities between the two would be a clear mistake. The importance of such effects remains to be measured, and this sort of measurement surely has a high priority in future research.

It must not be forgotten, however, that the empirical results of this study require heavy qualification. The experiments were few and limited in scope. They predate the war on poverty and Title I of the Elementary and Secondary Education Act—and thus the later knowledge gained and the change in society's commitment and attitudes. The sure conclusion to be drawn is that much more remains to be done in the way of careful measurement of the direct economic benefits resulting from straightforward improvements in education. Further work here is no less important than the study of complex interactions. It is also important to collect additional and more recent observations, especially on programs directly stimulated by current antipoverty legislation. Until these and other investigations are performed, benefit-cost analysis has little opportunity to give clear advice concerning particular improvements in education. This study suggests that one cannot assume complacently that any and all new educational expenditures yield returns far in excess of costs. It suggests as well that we should proceed with caution in our research and that the policy maker should employ the results of this study with caution.

APPENDIXES

Selection of Poverty Lines

Essays attempting to define poverty are numerous. Perhaps even more numerous are those reviewing past attempts at definition. Since the start of the official war on poverty, such discussions have become so common, and awareness of them so widespread, it is hardly necessary to review in detail the various possible approaches here.

Nevertheless, given the claims made for the system developed in Chapter 2, we must indicate why other approaches were not chosen. Only an impressionistic overview is attempted in order to show why it seemed compelling to follow the course outlined in Chapter 2. This discussion is followed by an attempt to tie up some of the loose ends of that theory.

Objective Approaches

No discussant in the poverty-line literature states outright that there is such a thing as an absolute definition of poverty. There are, however, strenuous attempts to make the definition as austerely objective as possible.

One technique is to specify a market basket of goods that appears to be essential for a reasonable standard of living. The size and contents of this basket vary a good deal among studies, and so do the names attached to the income level that permits the purchase of this market basket.[1] Sometimes two and even three lines are derived by the same study, each representing some particular degree of poverty and each labeled carefully to convey the appropriate connotation.

[1] For a sample see Gabriel Kolko, *Wealth and Power in America, An Analysis of Social Class and Income Distribution* (Praeger, 1962), pp. 100-02.

The wide disagreement on this issue has led most recent authors employing a market basket approach to admit frankly that it depends upon a heavy dose of value judgment, or that an attempt has been made to judge the appropriate size of a poverty-level basket in the same way most people would make the judgment.[2]

One way to avoid selecting items for a poverty-level market basket is to focus on one particular item that seems especially critical to health and welfare, decide what amount needs to be spent on that item, and then find out what income level is necessary to insure that a family does in fact manage to spend that requisite amount. This approach is the one used by Mollie Orshansky in deriving the poverty line of $3,000, the level most often used in discussions of poverty.[3] Her specific starting point is the dollar amount that must be spent on food in order to obtain a nutritionally adequate diet. She then determines what percentage of a "typical" budget is spent on food, and uses that to arrive at the answer that a $3,000 income is required for nutritive adequacy.

We might contrast this result with the work of Rose Friedman who uses the same general approach.[4] Her answer is that the poverty line is really closer to a $2,000 income. To pinpoint the source of this disagreement is not difficult. First, it should be noted that both agree on the amount of money required to purchase a nutritionally adequate diet, and that food must be the starting point because nutrition is the only consumer item where scientific standards of adequacy have been established.[5] Their only real difference is on the percentage of total family income that "should" be set aside for food.

Since the whole point of the exercise is to determine the total family income that separates poverty from nonpoverty, this percentage assumption is critically important. Orshansky assumes that 33 percent of the family income should be allocated for food since this is how the

[2] More detailed discussion on this approach can be found in Eugene Smolensky, "The Past and Present Poor," in Chamber of Commerce of the U.S.A., Task Force on Economic Growth and Opportunity, *The Concept of Poverty* (1965), pp. 35-68.

[3] Mollie Orshansky, "Counting the Poor: Another Look at the Poverty Profile," *Social Security Bulletin*, Vol. 28, No. 1 (January 1965), pp. 3-29; and her revised estimates in "Counting the Poor: Another Look at the Poverty Profile," reprinted in Louis A. Ferman, Joyce L. Kornbluh, and Alan Haber (eds.), *Poverty in America: A Book of Readings* (University of Michigan Press, 1965), pp. 48-82. In this second source a more sophisticated standard is used which includes, among other things, an adjustment for family size. The general approach is nevertheless the same.

[4] Rose D. Friedman, *Poverty: Definition and Perspectives* (Washington: American Enterprise Institute for Public Policy Research, 1965).

[5] Orshansky, in *Poverty in America*, p. 49; and Rose Friedman, *Poverty*, p. 15.

average family splits the budget. Thus, in order to find the total family income that just makes it to a nonpoverty level, the dollar amount required to buy an adequate diet should be multiplied by 3.[6] Friedman replies that "it appears difficult to justify using the multiplier applicable to all families to compute the income corresponding to a poverty level of living," and argues for a 60 percent allocation for food on the grounds that it is how *low income* families typically apportion their budgets.[7] This means that the amount required for food should be multiplied by 1.67 to derive the poverty line.

Neither author provides evidence or convincing logic as to why one multiplier rather than the other should be used. But if one is forced to choose, it might be noted that Friedman's criterion has some theoretical appeal: since we know nothing about the adequacy of nonfood expenditures, it might be assumed that poor families are more or less rational in their budget allocations and therefore would not allocate 60 percent of their income to food if that entailed cutbacks on expenditures that were more crucial than nutrition. Thus, if such studies were all we had to go on, a $2,000 poverty line would seem to be the more reasonable starting point for policy.

But this debate would, in any event, not seem very meaningful because of the arbitrary character of the dollar amount that was assumed necessary for food adequacy. This dollar amount describes the food expenditure that provides *three-fourths* of the families who make that dollar expenditure with *two-thirds* of the nutrition *recommended* by the Food and Nutrition Board of the National Research Council.[8] The two fractions are suggestions emanating from the Department of Agriculture, and neither Friedman nor Orshansky makes a serious attempt to defend these proportions. Moreover, it is not even clear what the "recommended" nutritional requirements mean. It might be thought that some physical impairment results if one fails to meet the standard. But then why does the Department of Agriculture say that two-thirds of the standard will do?

Perhaps the most interesting essays are those that start with a strong attack apparently scuttling any hope for a meaningful line, but conclude with specific line-drawing advice no less arbitrary than that given by authors who are not as openly distrustful. The most striking example of this is Dorothy Brady's juxtaposed comments on poverty lines:

---

[6] Orshansky, in *Poverty in America,* p. 49.
[7] Rose Friedman, *Poverty,* pp. 34-45.
[8] *Ibid.,* p. 22.

Theorists of all persuasions utilize such a concept implicitly while pro-
ponents of various types of social policy exploit the "poverty line" almost
melodramatically. Yet, when faced directly with the problem of determining
this measure for a given time and place, the theorist will deny the possibility
of a unique answer and the propagandist will settle for any one of many solutions if the result suits his purposes. . . .
    . . . the need for an objective approach, such as the "break even" point,
should be stressed. The break even point [is] the position on the income scale
at which average consumption exactly balances average income.[9]

Equally skeptical is Herman Miller who begins by saying "there is
no more agreement about who is poor than there is about what is
beautiful or ugly," and that this is "largely responsible for the wide
range that exists in estimates of the numbers of poor. . . ."[10] He later
argues that improved "minimum adequate" budget studies "must have
a high priority" because they can provide a "systematic approach to
the measurement of poverty . . . superior to the *ad hoc* definitions
that are in current use."[11]

The ambivalence of both these discussions demonstrates the intensity of the felt need to identify a poverty line. The discussion also
emphasizes that the call for objectivity helps little in securing agreement. Rather than suppressing this fact, it would seem wiser to admit
openly the inadequacy of objectivity. The admission leads to the observation that one's views of poverty are mostly a matter of subjective
preferences, and these must be interpreted politically in some way or
other.

Subjective Approaches

If the definition of poverty is largely a subjective matter, then there is
little reason why one individual's views on poverty have clear superiority over those of any other. This is not a very easy notion to live
with. The implication is that the definition of poverty, which is used

[9] Dorothy S. Brady, "Research on the Size Distribution of Income," in *Studies in
Income and Wealth* (National Bureau of Economic Research, 1951), Vol. 13, pp.
30-31. Among the shortcomings of Brady's measure is the unexplained exclusion
of contingency savings. It is difficult to argue that the "break even" point is more
"objective" than others; its only clear virtue is simplicity.
[10] Herman P. Miller, "Major Elements of a Research Program for the Study
of Poverty," in *Concept of Poverty*, p. 121.
[11] *Ibid.*, pp. 125-26.

for social policy purposes, must be the outcome of some sort of consensus; and it implies that we can never come to a consensus that entirely pleases a substantial percentage of the individuals who must enter into it. In this circumstance, the only unambiguous role for the "expert" is to describe clearly the sorts of living conditions that typically accompany various levels of income, thereby allowing a more knowledgeable decision on the part of the citizens (and their political representatives) who must enter into the compromise.

The belief that the definition of poverty has its roots in individual preferences suggests one other possible activity for students of poverty lines. That is to suggest the nature and shape of individual preferences. Such suggestions are hardly binding. Nevertheless, in the absence of a referendum, the theoretical analysis of individual preferences can help in constructing the approximate shape of what a "true" social consensus would be like.

Several recent approaches to the definition of poverty have gone all the way over to a purely subjective definition. And at least two have described in some detail how a poverty line can be systematically derived from the blending of individual opinions.

One of these systems, devised by Joseph S. Berliner, reasons from a very simple and straightforward starting point.[12] It states that an individual's personal definition of poverty is simply that income level where *he* would experience the sensation of being in poverty. In other words, the individual is hypothesized to imagine styles of life at various income levels and then to specify that level where he would sense that he is on the borderline between poverty and nonpoverty. Presumably the higher a person's present income level, the higher would be the hypothetical level where he would envision himself as experiencing poverty. From this, Berliner infers a socially determined policy line. This line is designated as the income level where individuals with slightly lower incomes would say that a slightly higher income level was necessary to put them on the borderline between poverty and nonpoverty, and that individuals immediately above would say that a slightly lower income level would put them on the borderline. Thus, if the present income of individuals is perfectly correlated with views on the borderline level of income, there would be one income group—and one only—who would say that the line separating poverty and nonpoverty is exactly the income level they now experience.

[12] Joseph S. Berliner and others, *Dependency and Poverty*, Colloquia: 1963-1964, The Florence Heller Graduate School for Advanced Studies in Social Welfare, Brandeis University (1965).

One peculiar implication of this "system" is that only the people in the immediate vicinity of the "socially determined" poverty line truly have a say in where it should be. It is also difficult to imagine what the individual should keep in mind when he answers the question, "I would feel in poverty if . . . ." Berliner gives no general psychological foundation for this answer. In essence, it is argued that the ordinary meaning of "poverty" is clear enough; hence no psychological specification is needed.

A more substantial psychic foundation is provided by Eugene Smolensky.[13] He argues that a typical citizen dislikes poverty because of the possibility that its ugliness may impinge upon the pleasantness of his own life. The eyesore of run-down slums is a recurring example. From this, however, it follows that we are not really concerned with low incomes per se, but only with some narrow range of secondary repercussions of poverty. It implies that we do not attack poverty per se but treat these secondary repercussions *directly*. Smolensky's suggestion that the poverty line should specify when these repercussions are reduced to an "acceptable" level seems to have no particular policy connotation. Moreover, Smolensky provides no explicit mechanism for determining the level of a line. His analysis emphasizes instead the rules for how fast this line travels upward over time.

Another approach is expressed by Victor Fuchs, who states:

> If it is true that the absence of poverty has a positive value for consumers, it may be asked why they do not purchase it directly, through philanthropy. . . . One answer is that the satisfaction derived from the absence of poverty can be enjoyed by everyone, like a bridge or a park or other public goods. There is no way for the purchaser to limit the enjoyment to himself as he would in the case of private goods. . . . Collective purchase through taxation may be the most rational way of satisfying this particular type of demand.[14]

Milton Friedman expresses a similar viewpoint:

> I am distressed by the sight of poverty; I am benefited by its alleviation; but I am benefited equally whether I or someone else pays for its alleviation; the benefits of other people's charity therefore partly accrue to me. To put it differently, we might all of us be willing to contribute to the relief of poverty, *provided* everyone else did. We might not be willing to contribute the same amount without such assurance.[15]

[13] Eugene Smolensky, "Investment in the Education of the Poor: A Pessimistic Report" (presented at the 1965 meeting of the American Economic Association), *American Economic Review*, Vol. 56, No. 2 (May 1966), pp. 370-78.

[14] Victor Fuchs, "Toward a Theory of Poverty," in *Concept of Poverty*, pp. 85-86.

[15] Milton Friedman, *Capitalism and Freedom* (University of Chicago Press, 1962), p. 191.

Neither Fuchs nor Friedman draws out the full implications of this position. The viewpoint does, however, have several obviously convenient properties; and it is a starting point similar to the one used in Chapter 2 of this study.

Among the properties of this approach are its focus on income levels per se and its provision of a psychological basis for this interest. Moreover, a definition of poverty based on such sympathies is not merely an abstract exercise. Along with the definition goes the implication that social action is called for. Nearly all discussions on poverty lines assume, at least implicitly, that the line does connote a social policy intent. Postulating that poverty level incomes cause displeasure for "all" citizens should provide a clear-cut basis for that implication.

Perhaps the most dubious aspect of this definition is that it hypothesizes a sympathy exactly opposite to an attitude commonly thought to be an important motivating force for the "economic man" of the twentieth century. This attitude might, in a word, be described as envy. Its implication is that income gains experienced by other individuals generally give rise to *negative* externalities.[16] But this does not rule out the possibility that income gains experienced by *some* outsiders give rise to positive externalities. And if such positive feelings arise for gains experienced by any identifiable category of people, this category would probably be those individuals who presently have exceedingly low incomes.

It seems reasonable to argue that most people regard income gains by others with some ambivalence. And it also seems reasonable to think that positive feelings are strongest when additional income is received by others who have relatively little income and that negative feelings are strongest when the others are relatively affluent. If this is the case, then the "top" poverty line, as defined in Chapter 2, should involve a very sharp demarcation for some individuals. At some income level, empathic concern not only vanishes but presumably would be replaced by hostility to further income advances.

Despite these observations, one might still take the cynical position that few people truly have altruistic sympathies in connection with any income gain experienced by *any* other person. It is true that the predominance of such sympathies has not been proven. But if one believes that altruistic concern is a very rare attitude, it is hard to be

---

[16] For the best known uses of this concept, see James S. Duesenberry, *Income Saving and the Theory of Consumer Behavior* (Harvard University Press, 1949); Arthur Ross, *Trade Union Wage Policy* (University of California Press, 1948); and J. de V. Graaff, *Theoretical Welfare Economics* (Cambridge University Press, 1957).

optimistic about the political tenability of fighting a war on poverty at meaningful levels. And, if this is the case, there is little point in worrying about the efficiency of alternative approaches to poverty alleviation.

Poverty Alleviation as a Public Good

The discussion in Chapter 2 suggests at several points that poverty alleviation, treated as a public good, is theoretically no more difficult to handle than the "usual" case of public goods. Two issues were ignored. The first was how a poor individual, who expects to be a beneficiary of an antipoverty program, will come to a decision about poverty definitions and the optimal level of antipoverty action. The second involves the double question of the appropriate distribution of the tax burden for antipoverty action and the derivation of a consensus line.

One might assume that a poor individual's views on poverty lines are summarized in saying "the higher the better." But, if we think of him as being no less socially conscious than the affluent citizen, we can at least expect him to provide reasonable answers to hypothetical questions where he is asked to submerge, for the moment, his hopes of personal gain. As far as the top poverty line is concerned, it does not seem peculiar to suppose that a poor citizen, as well as an affluent one, does not like to see other people in poverty. He would, of course, greatly prefer that he be lifted out of poverty along with the others who suffer from low incomes. But it is not totally out of the question that he would be willing to sacrifice at least a little in order to see many poor people benefit by a very great deal. Like the affluent citizen, he could specify the income level that is sufficiently high that he loses such inclinations altogether. If he does have such inclinations, it follows that he could also specify finite amounts of money he would pay to witness poor people, of a given income class, raised to a somewhat higher level of income. Continuing to think in this nonselfish mode, he should be able to arrive at a "bottom" poverty line similar in content to the one relating to a clearly affluent individual.

Two obvious qualifications must be added to this discussion. First, a poor individual may resent income gains experienced by his equally poor fellow citizen. This does not mean that he has an extraordinary lack of brotherly affection, but rather that income gains experienced by other poor people present a threat to his relative status. For an individual who is comfortably affluent, gains by very low income people represent no perceptible threat, though a salary raise awarded to his neighbor in suburbia may make an affluent citizen very unhappy.

A second obvious qualification is that a poor person does not, in reality, expect to sacrifice anything if a generous level is set for the "bottom" poverty line. An actual referendum determining social policy would present him with no conflicting motives and no obvious restraint in urging the most generous program possible. But this kind of situation appears in practically any example of public goods one might imagine. National defense, for instance, is frequently cited as a "pure" case of a public good (in the sense that it is supposedly consumed in equal amounts by all). But this does not mean that the owners and employees of the aerospace industry will conscientiously balance tax costs against the utility derived from added protection from aggressors. It is more likely that they are most intensely concerned with the possibilities of big government contracts. Thus, no decision about optimum spending on any public good can be expected to be entirely free of votes cast on the basis of vested interest.

How could a final and completely democratic consensus be arranged? The pure theory of public goods has an elegant solution which could be applied here without great modification.[17] The general idea of the solution in the standard public goods case is that individual citizens stipulate their social preferences in the form of demand curves. These are summed to establish the appropriate level of spending on the public good in question and taxes are allocated according to the individually specified demand curves. Since the demand curves represent how greatly valued are additionally purchased units of the public good, the tax allocation is arranged so that all individuals experience approximately the same net gain in welfare as a result of these purchases. In the ideal, the consensus is perfect and all parties to the decision end up in better positions.

Showing in detail how this theory can be applied to the case of poverty alleviation is, however, quite unnecessary. The practical difficulties involved in *any* public goods case are insurmountable, due mainly to the predictable lack of candor when an individual specifies his demand curve. In the case of poverty these difficulties would seem no more, and no less, difficult. As with other public goods, the most that can be hoped for is a rough-and-ready sort of consensus.

[17] Richard A. Musgrave, *The Theory of Public Finance* (McGraw-Hill, 1959), pp. 73-84; and Paul A. Samuelson, "Diagrammatic Exposition of a Theory of Public Expenditures," *Review of Economics and Statistics*, Vol. 37, No. 4 (November 1955), pp. 350-56.

APPENDIX B

Evaluation of Compensatory Education

Quantitative background information for the compensatory education programs discussed in Chapter 4 is summarized in Table B-1.

With the exception of Higher Horizons, this information is from generally uncirculated research reports (written under the auspices of the school districts) and from original material in the files of local boards of education. Information on the test score results discussed in the text is from the same sources.

For each of the compensatory education programs, test score information was available for both verbal and quantitative achievement. These were averaged together in the same fashion and with the same rationale as the Higher Horizons programs (see Chapter 4, pp. 67-71). A simple average in terms of yearly equivalent scores was used. No firm basis existed for a weighted averaging, and (as in the case of Higher Horizons) a weighted average giving somewhat heavier emphasis to verbal (or quantitative) scores would change very little the general conclusions. No two programs used exactly the same battery of tests. Some, at least in part, depended on locally devised testing instruments. Since these were generally administered throughout the school district, it was still possible to convert raw scores into yearly equivalents. The original research reports typically contained such conversions. Among nationally standardized tests used were the Gates Primary Reading Test; Iowa Test of Basic Skills; Lee-Clark Reading Readiness Test; Metropolitan Achievement Tests (tests from Primary, Elementary, and Intermediate batteries); Stanford Achievement Tests (Primary Battery and Intermediate Arithmetic); and STEP Reading Test. Ability and I.Q. tests of several varieties were also used for matching control and experimental groups and for observing if the programs had increased learning capacity. On the latter issue, no unambiguous gains were established in any of the programs examined.

TABLE B-1

Selected Data on Compensatory Education Programs

Program	Number of Experimental Schools Involved[a]	Number of Observed Pupils in Experimental Groups[b]	Observation Time (in months)[c]	Cost per Pupil for Observed Duration of Program[d]
Higher Horizons	18	1,101	22	$115
Program A	10	5,024	48	176
Program B	7	3,457	36	123
Program C	14	369	24	50
Program D	6	1,100	36	114
Program E	8	4,344	2[e]	160
Total	63	15,395	—	—

[a] Only 13 were separate junior high schools. The rest were elementary schools, though some of the research reports traced pupils in elementary school programs through to their performance in junior high schools. With the exception of Program E, all experiments utilized control schools of approximately the same number as the experimental schools. Program E relied exclusively on before-and-after comparisons and on comparisons with national norms.

[b] These were matched with control groups of approximately the same number. (Program E had no matching; see note a.) Matching was in terms of socioeconomic status and initial ability levels. Because different sampling procedures were used, numbers in this column do not accurately reflect the relative size of the programs. Some experiments observed pupils in nearly all grade levels affected by the program, others looked only at selected grade levels, and still others took a limited sample of pupils in selected grade levels. The number of schools involved is a better reflection of size.

[c] With two exceptions, this refers to the period elapsed between tests given at the beginning of the compensatory education and the latest (available) tests. Programs C and D did not conduct systematic pre-experiment testing; observation time was measured from the inception of the program to the time of last testing.

[d] Costs over and above the expense of the "regular" school program. These costs are probably slight underestimates since only costs that appear in the school budgets are included; this neglects (among other things) the expense incurred by agencies that cooperated with and supplemented the in-school programs.

[e] The total sample was tested immediately before and after a summer school program. A subsample of 150 pupils was selected for a follow-up study. These were reduced to 66 because of school transiency and other data retrieval problems, and the 66 were observed for an additional seven months.

The sample of compensatory education programs analyzed is small in relation to the number in existence during the time of the research. Two independent surveys performed during 1964-65 indicate that nearly 200 separate projects were then underway that dealt with school-age children and were considered to be accurately labeled as compensatory education. These projects came in many shapes and sizes; but, generally speaking, they appeared to employ the same sorts of techniques and were out to achieve the same sorts of goals as the six projects discussed in the text. Unfortunately, few of them had been carried on for very long, and few reported completed evaluations. Exploratory letters were sent to those reporting that some research had been completed but few useful replies were received.

Though there is no way to tell the extent or direction of possible bias in the six programs discussed, there are reasons to think they may have been of better than average quality. Reasonably good research was performed and available at each locale. In general, available research was the exception and not the rule. It seems reasonable, first of all, to suppose that programs that were relatively well organized in this aspect would also be relatively well administered. Second, knowledge on the part of the teachers and pupils that they were being systematically evaluated probably stimulated more conscientious behavior and resulted in more pronounced "Hawthorne effects." Third, as mentioned in the text, I was not permitted to examine several research reports, despite promising anonymity for them. Though I resisted the temptations of outright snooping, it was difficult to avoid the persistent rumors that the suppressed information indicated unfavorable outcomes for the compensatory education projects in question.

One of my major regrets is my failure to uncover any new clues about what mistakes to avoid and which approaches work best in a compensatory education program. Comparisons among the six programs yield very little, for they differed in too many ways. Among the major differences were: (1) level of costs; (2) method and quality of evaluation; (3) nature of the new technique, or techniques, being used; (4) size of the program; (5) degree of cultural deprivation among the pupils; and (6) the competence and enthusiasm of key administrators. On top of this, each of the programs attempted to institute several changes at once, and some autonomy was usually given to the individual schools to adopt unusual combinations or variants as they saw fit. Those individuals directly connected with the programs could offer only unsure (and sometimes conflicting) opinions on what made things tick (or not tick).

The Option Value of Education

For many people, one level of education is mainly of interest as a stepping stone to another level. The typical upper middle class teenager, for instance, would not be very interested in the news that graduating from high school means a good chance of his being hired at a steady job paying $4,000 a year. Rather, his sights are fixed on college, and probably graduate school, and the rewards he expects to flow from these. High school, to him, is simply a precondition. A teenager of less fortunate circumstances may also have yearnings to attend college. But because of tight financial circumstances, little social pressure, and the absence of intellectual stimulation at home, his attendance at college is neither guaranteed nor (quite possibly) is it something he is even sure he wants. Nevertheless, it is clear that he should not ignore the possibility; he may eventually go to college, and this opportunity should have some value to him. To take account of such circumstances, Burton Weisbrod has constructed a general formula to calculate what he calls the "option value" of education.[1]

While it seems apparent that some general formula is needed and desirable, there is some question whether the one derived by Weisbrod is entirely appropriate. This appendix first tries to show how the Weisbrod formulation may provide misleading policy advice; it then suggests an alternative formulation followed by a brief discussion on how the phenomena of option value might be blended into the empirical analysis appearing in the text.

The starting point of the Weisbrod formulation is an individual attempting to evaluate the worth of acquiring an additional incre-

---

[1] Burton A. Weisbrod, "Education and Investment in Human Capital," *Journal of Political Economy*, Vol. 70, No. 5, Supplement (October 1962), pp. 106-23; and Weisbrod, *External Benefits of Public Education: An Economic Analysis* (Princeton University, Department of Economics, Industrial Relations Section, 1964).

ment of formal schooling. It is argued that the individual should look not only at the rate of return he expects to earn if he completes that increment and then enters the labor market, but also at the opportunity to earn an additional rate of return if he decides to acquire still another increment (which is dependent on acquiring the first). Weisbrod argues that this additional rate of return, after adjustment by several factors, should be added to the rate of return for the first increment of education. It is suggested that this be done according to the following formula:

$$R_1 = R^*_1 + (R^*_2 - \overline{R})(C_2/C_1)(P_2)$$

where:

$R^*_1 = $ the rate of return if only the first level of education is completed

$R^*_2 = $ the rate of return on the second increment of education taken by itself

$\overline{R} = $ the "opportunity cost of expenditure on education in terms of the percentage return obtainable on the next best investment opportunity"

$C_2/C_1 = $ a weighting factor permitting the percentage returns on the costs of various levels to be added

$P_2 = $ the probability that a person who has attained the first educational level will go on to the second level.[2]

Thus, if (a) the anticipated rate of return to the first level (taken by itself) is 20 percent, (b) the anticipated rate of return to the second level (taken by itself) is 15 percent, (c) the opportunity cost of the "next best investment" is 5 percent, (d) the second level is twice as expensive as the first, and (e) the probability for attending the second level is exactly 0.5, then

$$R_1 = 0.20 + (0.15 - 0.05)(2/1)(1/2)$$
$$= 0.30.$$

Or, in other words, taking account of the option value yields a total

---

[2] "Education and Investment," pp. 109-10; and *External Benefits*, pp. 138-39. Weisbrod's original formulation is generalized to include any number of additional levels. Our reduction of the argument to only two levels of education makes the exposition easier without doing any serious disservice to the implications of the formula.

rate of return (R_1) for the first increment equal to 30 percent, as contrasted to the 20 percent figure derived without considering the possibility of acquiring the second educational increment.

Weisbrod goes on to apply this formula in several ways, most spectacularly in demonstrating that the rate of return for completing an elementary school education is over 50 percent higher than economists had thought it to be. Using actual estimates both for the rates of return to various educational levels and for the other elements in his formula, he argues that taking option values into account results in "increasing the return on elementary education from 35 to 54 percent."[3]

This result seems to have important consequences for the estimates in Chapters 4 and 5, many of which dealt with elementary school education. Weisbrod's result seems to hint that these estimates should be revised upward immediately by at least 50 percent. But that would be a very hasty conclusion. In the first place, Weisbrod is speaking exclusively in terms of school continuance; and, since Chapters 4 and 5 deal mainly with changes in educational quality, it is not clear that his results can be applied directly. Before discussing this possibility, let us examine how the Weisbrod formula might affect choices in the less involved context of school continuation decisions.

The heart of the Weisbrod formulation is the assumption (and use) of a given rate of return from the "next best investment opportunity." To see this clearly, things will be kept simple by continuing to assume that C_2/C_1 and P_2 cancel one another, as they did in our numerical example. It will also be supposed (as in our example) that R^*_1 is greater than R^*_2. This, it should be noted, is the "typical" case: all of Weisbrod's estimates, including the calculations for elementary school, involve lower rates of return for advanced increments of education.[4]

Let us now look more closely at the original numerical example

$$0.30 = 0.20 + (0.15 - 0.05).$$

A straightforward reading of this calculated relationship has a para-

---

[3] "Education and Investment," p. 112; and External Benefits, p. 141.

[4] Thus, Weisbrod's elementary school calculation was performed with Schultz's figures which estimate the following returns for the separate increments of education: elementary school graduation $= 35\%$, high school graduation $= 14\%$, and college graduation $= 9\%$. ("Education and Investment," p. 112; and External Benefits, p. 141.) Other applications of the formula can be found in these two sources and in Weisbrod, "On the Monetary Value of Education's Intergeneration Effects," Journal of Political Economy, Vol. 73, No. 6 (December 1965), pp. 643-49.

doxical connotation. Given the two incremental rates of return, it states that *if* the next best investment opportunity yields a 5 percent rate, *then* the individual investor would be willing to invest in the first increment even if he must forego an alternative investment yielding nearly 30 percent. Besides sounding a little odd, this observation does not appear to provide very useful information. The stipulation of the 5 percent rate already indicates that the individual's opportunity cost (for tying up funds in an educational investment) is 5 percent. Since the option value formulation simply moves the estimated rate of return from 20 to 30 percent, knowledge of the option value would have no influence on the decision to invest or not invest.[5]

Here it might be argued that the next best investment may yield more than 5 percent, and indeed might lie between 20 and 30 percent. If the yield on the next best investment does happen to be in this range, it might be thought that a calculation ignoring option values would indicate that the first level of education *should not* be undertaken, but a calculation including option values would suggest that it *should* be undertaken. This, however, is not the case. Should the yield on the next best investment be between 20 and 30 percent, the calculated value of the option would then fall below zero.[6] Indeed, as long as the next best alternative yields something in excess of 15 percent, it wipes out entirely the positive influence of the option value on the decision to invest in the first educational increment. Hence, the only time the option value does add a positive influence is when it is *not* needed; that is, when the next best investment pays less than 15 percent and consequently when the simple rate of return accruing from the first increment of education (20 percent) already tells the individual that this increment should be undertaken.[7]

If R^*_1 is in fact greater than R^*_2 (and the situations dealt with by

---

[5] Weisbrod never states *explicitly* that the option value does, or should, have an influence on educational investment decisions. Rather, he always puts the argument in terms of the danger of "undervaluing" a particular increment of education. Nevertheless, it is clear that if the option value is to be something more than an ornament, it must have an influence on decisions in some way or other.

[6] Weisbrod assumes that there is no obligation to actually undertake the additional increment of education. Thus, it can be said that the value of the option is merely zero when the value within the parentheses of the formula becomes negative ("Education and Investment," p. 111).

[7] Stated generally in terms of Weisbrod's symbols, the option value is positive only if $R^*_2 > \bar{R}$. But if $R^*_1 > R^*_2$, then $R^*_1 > \bar{R}$ any time the option value is positive, and the investment in the first increment would be undertaken even without cognizance of the option value.

Weisbrod are all of this variety), there seems to be only one way in which the option value could change someone's mind about investing in the first increment. And that is if rates of return on "the next best alternative investment" happen to decline over time. In other words, the payoff rate on other investments (or the interest rate on borrowed funds) must fall during the interval between the first and second educational increments. While some individuals may experience such a decline in relevant interest rates, no economic principle comes to mind as to why this should be the general rule.[8]

The above analysis would apply with equal relevance and with similar implications to social policy decisions. If the R's represent social rates of return and R^*_1 is greater than R^*_2 for two successive increments of education, there appears to be little reason why knowledge of the option value should alter social decisions about whether or not to encourage students to continue through the first increment of schooling. As in the conclusions above, the option value is positive only when R^*_1 and $\overline{R}$ already indicate that further investment should be undertaken in the first educational increment.

What about the situation where the second educational increment yields a higher rate of return than the first? Though Weisbrod makes no calculations for circumstances of this type, he does observe that his formula is applicable in such a situation. And, when rates *do* rise with successive increments, it is easy to demonstrate that the option value formula could weigh heavily in an individual's decision about undertaking the first increment. Thus, if we alter the numerical example by simply imagining a 3 percent return on the first increment, the outcome would be

$$R_1 = 0.03 + (0.15 - 0.05)$$
$$= 0.13.$$

This suggests that an individual would be willing to undertake the investment even though $\overline{R}$ is greater than R^*_1. If he had ignored the option value component, it is clear he would have rejected investment

[8] It might also be argued that uncertainty could give the option a meaningful role even if $R^*_1 > R^*_2$. Thus, even if the individual investor thinks that his situation is as described in the numerical example and that his interest cost ($\overline{R}$) will remain constant over time, there is always the possibility that some (or all) of these expectations will not materialize. This in turn implies that he might be willing to pay a premium for an educational increment that does have a further option. But this premium cannot be determined simply by looking at expected rates of return. And it is surely not determined by calculations using the Weisbrod formula.

in the first increment on the grounds that the next best investment opportunity provided a higher rate of return. The recognition of the option value tips the scales. It raises the overall expected rate of return above the opportunity cost of missing the next best investment opportunity of 5 percent.

Thus, the option value can have a clearly positive influence, without the special requirement that the rates on alternative investment opportunities fall over time. The formula, in this instance, seems to provide the right sort of advice to an individual investor.

If, however, we turn to the question of social policy, the option value must be interpreted more cautiously. If social policy is faced with the same configuration of rates specified in the immediately preceding example, in which $R_1 = 0.13 = 0.03 + (0.15 - 0.05)$, this would seem to state that encouraging and supporting students to complete the first increment is a wise policy. The 13 percent rate exceeds the "next best opportunity" of 5 percent. But should the comparison really occur with the 5 percent rate? Why not also consider the rate of return comparison between investing in the first increment and investing in the second? For the individual investor, a choice of this kind is out of the question because he must complete the initial increment before he can enter the second. Social policy, on the other hand, can presumably increase the flows of pupils through higher levels of education just as easily as it can increase flows through lower levels. For instance, it would seem quite feasible to significantly increase the number of high school graduates attending college without doing anything about the dropout rate from high school.[9] Investment in the first level will, of course, imply some additional people going through the second increment as they take advantage of their option. But this would seem not nearly so profitable as devoting our attention directly to increasing the rate at which people achieve the second increment. Supporting addi-

[9] One way to conceptualize this is in terms of Weisbrod's P values, which relate to the actual proportions of students—completing a previous increment of education—who go on to the next higher increment. Social policy aimed at increasing flows through a given level can be thought of (in Weisbrod's terms) as varying the value of P relating to that level. Since Weisbrod deals only with the payoffs for school continuation, varying the P's—and thereby varying the flows through various educational levels—is the only policy change to which the payoff rates directly apply. His formulation also implies that flows through various levels can be increased at will, without any "extra" costs incurred in the process of persuading students to continue. For the time being, our analysis is similarly limited to the discussion of "costless" changes in the flows of students at different levels.

tional students through the first increment of education would not, therefore, be the best use of added funds for social investment.

As long as social policy decisions keep in mind the alternative of supporting heavier student flows through any increment of schooling, it appears that the option value formula has no danger of providing misleading information. But consider the following situation:

$$R_1 = 0.08 + (0.15 - 0.05)$$
$$= 0.18.$$

This suggests that increasing flows through the first level is not only more profitable than the 5 percent noneducation alternative, but also more profitable than increasing flows through the upper level. The overall rate of return for investing in the first increment is calculated at 18 percent as compared to the 15 percent rate for the second increment. This implies that new investments should be directed toward supporting students through the first level where some students earn as little as an 8 percent rate and some earn an additional 15 percent. This appears more profitable than increasing flows where all students earn a 15 percent rate. The implied policy advice in this circumstance seems very peculiar indeed.

To derive a formula that avoids the problems just discussed, let us first deal in the simple terms of investments that yield immediate pay-offs and thus require no adjustment for time preferences. With this simplifying assumption, the rate of return on any educational increment can be expressed as

$$R^*_j = B'_j / C_j$$

where C_j represents the cost of the increment and B'_j represents the net gain in income (that is, total income gain minus the costs of the investment). For those individuals who end up acquiring *only* the first increment of an educational sequence, the overall rate of return can be expressed as

$$R^*_1 = B'_1 / C_1.$$

For those individuals who end up acquiring both the first and second increments, the overall rate of return can be expressed as

$$R^*_{(1,2)} = \frac{B'_1 + B'_2}{C_1 + C_2}.$$

In other words, the two educational increments can be treated as one with an overall rate of return $(R^*_{(1,2)})$ representing the total net income gain as a percentage of total costs.

If the individual contemplating the investment in the first educational increment knows that he has a probability (P_2) of being among those students who do go on to acquire the second increment of education, it can be said that his probable net benefits are

$$B_1(1 - P_2) + (B_1 + B_2)P_2.$$

His probable costs can be stated in similar fashion. And his expected overall rate of return for committing himself to the first increment of education can be described as

$$R_1 = \frac{B'_1(1 - P_2) + (B'_1 + B'_2)P_2}{C_1(1 - P_2) + (C_1 + C_2)P_2}.$$

For the individual investor this formula can be used in generally the same way as the original Weisbrod formula. If the rate of return is larger for the first increment than for the second, the option value can be safely neglected. R_1 compared with the rate of interest on the next best investment would be sufficient information. If the rate on the first increment is larger, the probable rate of return (taking the option value into account) would state correctly the relevant alternative rate of interest at which the individual would be indifferent about investing or not investing in the educational increment. On this rate of interest, it can be shown that the above formulation and the original Weisbrod formulation are in general agreement.

The main proviso of the formula advanced here is that the alternative rate of interest on the "next best" investment opportunity is the same for undertaking both the first and second educational increments. Individual investors may, of course, experience changes over time in the attractiveness of their investment alternatives, and the formula could be adjusted for this. But in the case of social policy decisions—the focus of the analysis in the text—it seems safe to assume that the interest rate on alternative social investments (or the opportunity cost of tax money) does not change during the relatively brief time period between educational increments undertaken for a given wave of students.

Looking now at the implications for social policy decisions, it seems clear that our new formula does not yield the puzzling sorts of answers the original Weisbrod formula was capable of generating. In particular, if rates of return rise with successive increments of schooling, the formula just developed can never generate the result that investment in the first increment of education gives rise to a higher overall rate of return than does investment in the second increment.[10]

Thus, for social policy, it appears sufficient to know simply the separate rates of return for each educational increment. This would be enough information for specifying the point where it is most profitable to increase the flow of students. This in turn seems to say that the formula just devised (as well as the Weisbrod formula) has no real interest for social policy decisions.

One can, however, imagine various constraints and conditions under which it *would* be of interest. For instance, it might not be possible to increase flows through a given increment without undertaking substantial costs in the counseling and persuasion of new recruits for this increment. In this case, even if this increment pays a higher rate of return than all earlier investments, it might be more efficient to increase flows through one of the earlier levels (presuming this requires little extra costs for counseling, etc.) in the anticipation that some of these students, without additional prompting, will voluntarily undertake the latter increment which pays the relatively high rate of return. But this case would not seem to arise very often in

---

[10] To prove this, note that B'_2/C_2 can be rewritten as

$$\frac{B'_2\left(\dfrac{C_1}{C_2} + 1\right)}{C_2\left(\dfrac{C_1}{C_2} + 1\right)} = \frac{B'_2\left(\dfrac{C_1}{C_2}\right) + B'_2}{C_1 + C_2}.$$

Also note that if $B'_1/C_1 < B'_2/C_2$, then $B'_1 < B'_2 C_1/C_2$. It follows that

$$\frac{B'_1 + B'_2}{C_1 + C_2} < \frac{B'_2\left(\dfrac{C_1}{C_2}\right) + B'_2}{C_1 + C_2}$$

and

$$\frac{B'_1 + B'_2}{C_1 + C_2} < \frac{B'_2}{C_2}.$$

The left-hand side of this last expression is the expected overall rate of return (R_1) for undertaking the first increment of education when the probability (P_2) is 1 that the second increment will be undertaken. There is no trouble demonstrating that a probability less than this would only reinforce the conclusion.

practice. (Why should it be relatively harder to tempt an individual to undertake a relatively higher paying increment of education?)

A more likely situation, amenable to the application of this formula, is that characterized by many of the observations in Chapters 4 and 5. There we dealt often with the changes in costs per student and in curriculum.[11] In these instances, the only tangible basis on which to estimate returns consisted of changes in test scores indicating that more was learned and therefore that more would be earned during adult working lives. There is, however, a good possibility that the experience of measurably improved education at an early level will influence some individuals to continue their formal schooling for a longer period of time. The short-run evidence actually observed gave no firm clues along these lines; nonetheless, the assumption of some school continuance effects seems eminently reasonable and may very likely be borne out by longer run observations.

To take an example derived from magnitudes calculated in Chapters 3 and 4, suppose that a "compensatory education" program in elementary school has roughly the same efficiency as did the Higher Horizons program in raising test scores, and suppose also that the later effects on high school dropout rates are similar to those described by Weisbrod in his St. Louis case study.[12] In order to make this example coincide with the calculations in the text, it is advisable to work things through in terms of a benefit-cost ratio. Our formula can be suitably altered to read

$$(B/C)_1 = \frac{B_1(1 - P_2) + (B_1 + B_2)P_2}{C_1(1 - P_2) + (C_1 + C_2)P_2}$$

where B_1 represents the average income gain (gross of costs) associated with the observed gain in actual learning; B_2 represents the added income gain (gross of costs) experienced by those individuals who are deterred from dropping out of high school (as a result of the compensatory education program); P_2 represents the estimated proportion of students who are deterred; C_1 represents the per student costs of the compensatory education program; and C_2 represents the total costs (direct costs plus foregone earnings) for the last two years of high school education. Suppose also that all dollar amounts have been appropriately discounted so that $(B/C)_1$ represents the present value of expected benefits over costs.

[11] See pp. 61-99.
[12] See pp. 55-60 and 70-72.

Reasonable replacements for the symbols would result in something like the following:

$$(B/C)_1 = \frac{(200)\,(0.96) + (200 + 5000)\,(0.04)}{(300)\,(0.96) + (300 + 2000)\,(0.04)}.$$

All dollar values are convenient approximations of magnitudes derived from the Higher Horizons program and the St. Louis dropout program. It is assumed that 4 percent more students complete high school than would have if the compensatory education had not occurred. This is estimated on the basis that the St. Louis program brought about an apparent "rescue rate" of 8 percent, and it cost about twice as much as the assumed expense for the compensatory education being dealt with in the present example. Working through the arithmetic reveals that

$$(B/C)_1 = \frac{410}{380} = 1.08.$$

Thus, if it is thought that some pupils simply learn more during the compensatory education period without any influence on their duration in school, while others experience not only this but also the added learning of two extra years of high school, the benefit-cost ratio relating to the advisability of the compensatory education program can be calculated as above. The result in this particular example turns out to be a little greater than 1.

If, on the other hand, one viewed the program *solely* as an attempt to increase the amount immediately learned, or *solely* as a dropout prevention program, then the benefit-cost ratio would be estimated to be less than 1. For a narrow focus exclusively on the amount learned, the ratio would come out to 0.67 (or 200 ÷ 300). Viewed solely as a dropout prevention program and neglecting all increases in immediate learning, the ratio would be 0.53 = 5000(0.04)/[300 + 2000(0.04)].

The results of this calculation are striking and present a serious apparent threat to many of the calculations in the text. Nevertheless, it is important to keep in mind the following caveats:

1. The St. Louis dropout prevention program concentrated exclusively on school continuation; it dealt only with individuals labeled as potential dropouts and there were indications that it operated at more than the usual level of efficiency.

2. Some compensatory education experiments did search for short-

run clues on inclinations to remain in school, but nothing substantial was discovered.

3. The evidence from the Project Talent survey indicates that dropout rates are peculiarly higher in relatively expensive schools.

It must therefore be concluded that, while it might be true that some dropouts were in fact "saved" by the programs examined in Chapter 4, it is unlikely that this effect is nearly as strong as the above calculation would imply. Before any firm idea can be had on what the magnitudes really are, detailed longitudinal studies are required.

Bibliography

Becker, Gary S. *Human Capital.* New York: National Bureau of Economic Research, 1964.

Bloom, Benjamin S. *Stability and Change in Human Characteristics.* New York: John Wiley & Sons, 1964.

Bloom, Benjamin S., Allison Davis, and Robert Hess. *Compensatory Education for Cultural Deprivation.* Chicago: Holt, Rinehart & Winston, 1965.

Borus, Michael E. "A Benefit-Cost Analysis of the Economic Effectiveness of Retraining the Unemployed," *Yale Economic Essays,* Vol. 4, No. 2 (Fall 1964), pp. 371-430.

Clark, Kenneth. *Dark Ghetto.* New York: Harper & Row, 1965.

Coleman, James S., and others. *Equality of Educational Opportunity.* Washington: Government Printing Office, 1966.

Conant, James B. *Slums and Suburbs.* New York: McGraw-Hill, 1961.

Corazzini, Arthur J. "Prevention of High School Dropouts: An Analysis of Costs and Benefits." Mimeographed. Princeton University, 1965.

Cutright, Phillips. "A Pilot Study of Factors in Economic Success and Failure Based on Selective Service and Social Security Records." Mimeographed. U.S. Department of Health, Education, and Welfare, Social Security Administration, 1964.

Detroit High School Leaver Project. Detroit: Michigan Employment Security Commission, Detroit Board of Education, October 1964.

Flanagan, John C., and others. *The American High School Student.* Technical Report to U.S. Office of Education, Cooperative Research Project 635. University of Pittsburgh, Project Talent Office, 1964.

———. *Designing the Study.* Technical Report to U.S. Office of Education, Cooperative Research Project 566. University of Pittsburgh, Project Talent Office, 1960.

———. *Studies of the American High School.* Technical Report to U.S. Office of Education, Cooperative Research Project 226. University of Pittsburgh, Project Talent Office, 1962.

Fleisher, Belton M. "The Effect of Income on Delinquency," *American Economic Review,* Vol. 56, No. 1 (March 1966), pp. 118-37.

Friedman, Milton. *Capitalism and Freedom.* Chicago: University of Chicago Press, 1962.

Fuchs, Victor R. "Toward a Theory of Poverty," in Chamber of Commerce of the U.S.A., *The Concept of Poverty.* Washington: Chamber of Commerce of the U.S.A., Task Force on Economic Growth and Opportunity, 1965, pp. 69-92.

Gallaway, Lowell E. "The Foundations of the 'War on Poverty,' " *American Economic Review,* Vol. 55, No. 1 (March 1965), pp. 122-30.

Goldstein, Leo S. "Evaluation of an Enrichment Program for Socially Disadvantaged Children." Mimeographed. New York Medical College, Institute for Developmental Studies, June 1965.

Green, Christopher. *Negative Taxes and the Poverty Problem.* Washington: Brookings Institution, 1967.

Hanoch, Giora. "Rates of Return, 1960." Paper No. 6428. Unpublished. University of Chicago, Office of Agricultural Research, November 12, 1964.

Hansen, W. Lee. "Total and Private Rates of Return to Investment in Schooling," *Journal of Political Economy,* Vol. 71, No. 2 (April 1963), pp. 128-40.

Harcourt, Brace and World, Inc. *Test Data Reports.* Nos. 1-44. New York: Harcourt, Brace & World, 1964.

HARYOU (Harlem Youth Opportunities Unlimited). *Youth in the Ghetto.* New York: HARYOU, 1964.

Kiesling, Herbert J. "Measuring a Local Government Service: A Study of Efficiency of School Districts in New York State." Ph.D. dissertation, Harvard University, 1965.

Lampman, Robert J. "Approaches to the Reduction of Poverty," *American Economic Review,* Vol. 55, No. 2 (May 1965), pp. 521-29.

Miller, Herman P. "Lifetime Income and Economic Growth," *American Economic Review,* Vol. 55, No. 4 (September 1965), pp. 834-44.

Miller, S. Michael, and Martin Rein. "The War on Poverty: Perspectives and Prospects," in Ben B. Seligman (ed.), *Poverty as a Public Issue.* New York: Free Press, 1965, pp. 272-320.

Morgan, James, and Charles Lininger. "Education and Income: Comment," *Quarterly Journal of Economics,* Vol. 78, No. 2 (May 1964), pp. 346-47.

Morgan, James N., Martin H. David, Wilbur J. Cohen, and Harvey E. Brazer. *Income and Welfare in the United States.* New York: McGraw-Hill, 1962.

Musgrave, Richard A. *The Theory of Public Finance.* New York: McGraw-Hill, 1959.

Orshansky, Mollie. "Counting the Poor: Another Look at the Poverty Profile," *Social Security Bulletin,* Vol. 28, No. 1 (January 1965), pp. 3-29. Reprinted in Louis A. Ferman, Joyce L. Kornbluh, and Alan Haber (eds.), *Poverty in America: A Book of Readings.* Ann Arbor: University of Michigan Press, 1965, pp. 48-82.

Page, David A. "Retraining Under the Manpower Development Act: A Cost-Benefit Analysis," *Public Policy,* Vol. 13 (1964), pp. 257-67. Brookings Reprint 86.

Project Talent Data Bank, a National Data Bank for Research in Education and the Behavioral Sciences. University of Pittsburgh.

Riessman, Frank. *The Culturally Deprived Child.* New York: Harper & Row, 1962.

Samuelson, Paul A. "Diagrammatic Exposition of a Theory of Public Expenditures," *Review of Economics and Statistics,* Vol. 37, No. 4 (November 1955), pp. 350-56.

Schultz, Theodore W. "Capital Formation by Education," *Journal of Political Economy,* Vol. 68 (December 1960), pp. 571-83.

———. "Education and Economic Growth," in Nelson B. Henry (ed.), *Social Forces Influencing American Education.* Chicago: University of Chicago Press, 1961.

———. "Investing in Poor People: An Economist's View," *American Economic Review,* Vol. 55, No. 2 (May 1965), pp. 510-20.

Somers, Gerald G., and Ernst W. Stromsdorfer. "A Benefit-Cost Analysis of Manpower Retraining," in Gerald G. Somers (ed.), *Proceedings of the Seventeenth Annual Meeting,* Industrial Relations Research Association. Madison, Wisconsin, 1965, pp. 172-85.

Tobin, James. "On Improving the Economic Status of the Negro," *Dædalus,* Vol. 94, No. 4 (Fall 1965), pp. 878-98.

U.S. Bureau of the Census. "Educational Attainment," *U.S. Census of Population: 1960.* PC(2)-7B. Washington: Government Printing Office, 1963.

———. "Occupation by Earnings and Education," *U.S. Census of Population: 1960.* PC(2)-7B. Washington: Government Printing Office, 1963.

U.S. Congress, Senate Committee on Labor and Public Welfare. *The War on Poverty: The Economic Opportunity Act of 1964.* A Compilation of Materials Relevant to S. 2642. Document No. 86. 88 Cong. 2 sess. Washington: Government Printing Office, 1964.

———. *Elementary and Secondary Education Act of 1965*. Report No. 146. 89 Cong. 1 sess. Washington: Government Printing Office, 1965.

U.S. Department of Labor. *Manpower Report of the President and a Report on Manpower Requirements, Resources, Utilization, and Training, 1966*. Washington: Government Printing Office, 1966.

U.S. Office of the President. *Economic Report of the President, January 1964, Together with the Annual Report of the Council of Economic Advisers*. Washington: Government Printing Office, 1964.

———. *Economic Report of the President, January 1966, Together with the Annual Report of the Council of Economic Advisers*. Washington: Government Printing Office, 1966.

Weikert, David E., Constance Kamii, and others. "Perry Preschool Project Progress Report." Mimeographed. Ypsilanti, Michigan: Ypsilanti Public Schools, June 1964.

Weisbrod, Burton A. "Education and Investment in Human Capital," *Journal of Political Economy*, Vol. 70, No. 5, Supplement (October 1962), pp. 106-23.

———. "Preventing High School Dropouts," in Robert Dorfman (ed.), *Measuring Benefits of Government Investments*. Washington: Brookings Institution, 1965, pp. 117-49.

———. *External Benefits of Public Education: An Economic Analysis*. Princeton: Princeton University, Department of Economics, Industrial Relations Section, 1964.

Weisbrod, Burton A., and William J. Swift. "On the Monetary Value of Education's Intergeneration Effects," *Journal of Political Economy*, Vol. 73, No. 6 (December 1965), pp. 643-49.

INDEX

Achievement tests, standardized: compensatory education programs, 67, 73-75, 139; Higher Horizons program, 67; preschool programs, 79n, 80n, 81n; Project Talent survey, 85, 86, 88
Anderson, W. H. Locke, 19n
Antipoverty education: comparison of types, 35; effects of large amounts, 108-12; equal opportunity, 117-18; external benefits, 119; payoff rates, 16, 96-99, 127-28; policy conclusions, 125-29; second generation gains, 101-07; summary of benefits, 124. See also Compensatory education; Higher Horizons program; Job retraining; Preschool training; Project Talent survey
Antipoverty goals, 13, 33; nonpecuniary considerations, 113-14, 119-22, 124-28. See also Antipoverty education; Transfer payments
Area Redevelopment Act, 38

Becker, Gary S., 4, 57, 58n, 70, 123n
Benefit-cost analysis of educational programs: discount rate, 37-38; tax costs, 36, 37; technique used, 1, 2, 21-24, 30-32
Benefit-cost estimates: compensatory education, 75-77; delinquency reduction, 120-22; dropout prevention, 52, 53, 54n, 56; Higher Horizons program, 69-72; increased expenditures, 91; job retraining, 40, 47, 49, 50; preschool programs, 80; Project Talent survey, 91-96, 128
Bloom, Benjamin, S., 7n, 15n, 69n
Borus, Michael E., 39n
Bridgman, Donald S., 12n

Capital investments, 3-8
Carver, Thomas N., 108n
CED. See Committee for Economic Development

Clark, Kenneth B., 7n, 62n, 118n
Coleman, James S., 91n
College education: payoff rate, 10-11
Committee for Economic Development (CED), 9n, 18n, 108n, 116n
Compensatory education: benefit-cost estimates, 69-72, 75-77; Higher Horizons program, 63-67; programs providing, 63-67, 72-74; short-run findings, 74, 77; size of programs, 140; tests used, 139. See also Demonstration Guidance Project; Higher Horizons program; Preschool training
Conant, James R., 15n
Connecticut job retraining case study, 39-50
Corazzini, Arthur J., 59n
Cultural deprivation, 61-62. See also Juvenile delinquency; Slum schools; Socioeconomic status
Cutright, Phillips, 12n

David, Martin, 11n, 54n
Davis, Allison, 7n
Demonstration Guidance Project, 62
Denison, Edward F., 13n
Dentler, Robert A., 107n
Direct-subsidy programs. See Transfer payments
Discount rate, 37-38
Dorfman, Robert, 38n
Dropout prevention, 14, 15, 51; St. Louis case study findings, 53, 59. See also School continuance
Dropouts: expected earnings, 23; Higher Horizons program, 65; Project Talent survey, 87, 92; rates, 107n
Dunlop, John T., 18n

Eckaus, R. S., 10n
Eckstein, Otto, 37n, 38n
Economic growth, 122-24
Economic Opportunity Act, 61
Education, influence of: external bene-